RURAL NON-FARM SECTOR

RURAL NON-FARM SECTOR

A. SHANMUGASUNDARAM

K. RAVICHANDRAN

A. SAVARIMUTHU

ABHIJEET PUBLICATIONS

DELHI 110094

ABHIJEET PUBLICATIONS
2/46 Tukhmeerpur Extension
Delhi-110 094
Phone: 011-22960492 (Fax), 65698474
E-mail: abhijeetpublication@gmail.com

RURAL NON-FARM SECTOR

First Published 2008

ISBN 978-81-89886-74-5

PRINTED IN INDIA

Published by J.K. Singh for Abhijeet Publications, Delhi-110 094, Lasertypeset by Gaurav Graphics, New Delhi and Printed at Himanshu Printers, Delhi.

Preface

Institutionalization of rural credit started in India with the enactment of first Cooperative Credit Societies Act of 1904. Since then, Primary Agricultural Cooperative Societies were organized to provide short term and medium term credit to farmers. Later, a separate agency to provide long term credit to the farmers for redemption of their prior debts and for making permanent improvement on lands was felt, which resulted in the establishment of Land Mortgage Banks (LMB). The recommendations of All India Rural Credit Survey Committee (AIRCSC) in 1954 changed nomenclature of the banks from land 'mortgage' banks to land 'development' banks (LDBs). Over a period of time the Long Term Cooperative Credit Structure (LTCCS) was reviewed by number of Committees and Commissions.

Meantime the potentialities of Rural Non-Farm Sector in generating employment and income in rural areas not only attracted the policy makers, but also attracted the LDBs. This trend has again changed the nomenclature of these banks as Agricultural and Rural Development Banks (ARDBs). This study is an attempt to analyze the role of PCARDBs in the promotion of RNFS as well as the potentialities of RNFS in the strengthening of business of PCARDBs in the study area. Two districts in Tamil Nadu namely Dindugal and Nagapattinam were chosen purposively for this study. Many people have contributed for the successful completion of this study. It is our duty to record our sincere thanks to all of them.

We record our sincere thanks to Rt. Rev. Dr. T. ARULDOSS, Bishop of Tranquebar and Secretary of TBML College for his blessings. We express our sincere thanks to Dr. G. JONAS GUNASEKARAN, Principal, TBML College Porayar for his support and encouragement for the completion of this study.

We thank Dr. V. FRANK RATNAKUMAR, Vice Principal, TBML College, Porayar for his valuable guidance, advice and care, without which, it would not have been possible for us to complete this work. We place on record our gratitude to our Gurus Dr. S. NAKKIRAN former Principal, and Dr. S. RAMAMOORTHY, former Professor of Tamil for their guidance, support and encouragements.

Our gratitude and thanks are due to Dr. A. SAKKARAVEL, Former Principal, Poombuhar College, Melaiyur, Dr. A. WILLIAM ROBERTSON Reader and Head, Department of Cooperation and to Dr. A. RAJAN, Reader and Head Department of Commerce (Rted.), TBML College Porayar for their encouragement and valuable suggestions in the completion of this study.

We express our sincere gratitude to Dr. S.P. SHANMUGAM, Librarian (Rted.), Mr.W. SELVARAJ ISSAC, Physical Director (Rted.), Dr. S. SUKUMAR, Reader in Cooperation, Mr. GEORGE D. PETER, former Professor of English, TBML College Porayar, Dr. M. SUYAMBULINGAM, Retired Professor, Tamilnadu Agricultural University, Coimbatore and Dr. A. ARIVOLI, Reader, Department of Chemistry, Rajas College, Pudukottai, for all sorts of help they extended whenever we approached.

Our thanks are due to the Special Officers, Secretaries and Team of Employees of sample PCARDBs in Dindugal and Nagapattinam districts for their non tiring help in providing data for our research work.

We thank Mr. S. AZHAGERSAMY, MCA., Amirtham Xerox, Porayar, who helped us in bring out the script.

We record our thanks to M/S Abhijeet Publications, New Delhi for their sincerity in bringing out this script in book form.

AUTHORS

Contents

Contents

List of Tables

List of Charts

List of Boxes

List of Diagrams

List of Abbreviations Used

ACRC	Agriculture Credit Review Committee
AEZ	Agriculture Export Zone
AIRCSC	All India Rural Credit Survey Committee
ARDBs	Agriculture and Rural Development Banks
ARDC	Agricultural Refinance and Development Corporation
BC	Backward Class
CBs	Commercial Banks
CRAFICARD	Committee to Review Arrangements for Institutional Credit for Agriculture and Rural Development
DCCB	District Central Cooperative Bank
DDCCB	Dindugal District Central Cooperative Bank
DIC	District Industries Centre
DRDA	District Rural Development Agency
DRIP	District Rural Industries Project
EDP	Entrepreneurship Development Programme
EOU	Export Oriented Unit
FGD	Focus Group Discussion
GDDP	Gross District Domestic Product
GDP	Gross Domestic Product
GLC	Ground Level Credit
GRU	Gandhigram Rural University
KCCB	Kumbakonam Central Cooperative Bank
KVIB	Khadi and Village Industries Board
KVIC	Khadi and Village Industries Commission
KVIs	Khadi and Village Industries

LDBs	Land Development Banks
LMBs	Land Mortgage Banks
LTCCS	Long Term Cooperative Credit Structure
MBC	Most Backward Class
NABARD	National Bank for Agriculture and Rural Development
NCAER	National Council for Applied Economic Research
NFE	Non Farming Employment
NFS	Non-Farm Sector
NGOs	Non Governmental Oraganisations
NPA	Non Performing Assets
NSDP	Net State Domestic Product
PACBs	Primary Agriculture Cooperative Banks
PACS	Primary Agriculture Cooperative Societies
PCARDBs	Primary Cooperative Agriculture and Rural Development Banks
PLDBs	Primary Land Development Banks
PMRY	Prime Minister's Rozgar Yojana
PRA	Participatory Rural Appraisal
RBI	Reserve Bank of India
RCS	Registrar of Cooperative Societies
REGP	Rural Employment Guarantee Programme
RFE	Rural Farming Employment
RNFE	Rural Non Farming Employment
RRBs	Regional Rural Banks
SC	Schedule Caste
SCARDBs	State Cooperative Agriculture and Rural Development Banks
SCB	State Cooperative Bank
SGSY	Swarnajayanthi Gram Swarozgar Yojana
SHGs	Self Help Groups
SIDCO	Small Industries Development Corporation
SIPCOT	Small Industries Promotion Corporation of Tamilnadu
SISI	Small Industries Service Institute
SRTO	Small Road Transport Operations
SSI	Small Scale Industries
STCCS	Short Term Cooperative Credit Structure
TNSCARDB	Tamil Nadu State Cooperative Agriculture and Rural Development Bank
TVEs	Township and Village Enterprises
UTP	Union Territory of Pondicherry

1

Rural Non-Farm Sector

Agriculture is still one of the predominant forms of economic activities in India. It provides employment to 58 per cent of the work force and contributes around 25 per cent to the Gross Domestic Product (GDP). The role of the agricultural sector as an employment and income provider to growing labour force has slowly been coming down over the years, which attracted the attention of policy makers (Usha Tuteja; 2004). Nowadays unemployment in the rural areas has become the major contributing factor for high incidence of poverty. In order to tackle this situation development of Non-Farm Sector (NFS), which has potential for generation of sizable number of employment opportunities in the rural areas, assumes greater importance. NFS is very much essential to achieve our national objective of integrated rural development, as it facilitates to provide either supplementary or alternative sources of income to the poor agriculturists. NFS is an enterprise and artisanal units which could be classified as small, tiny, village cottage and household units involved in manufacturing, procuring, preserving and storing or marketing of goods can be grouped under this head. Those engaged in services which could be considered capable of generating employment opportunities to the rural work force without a major shift in their habitat can also be brought under the category of NFS. On the basis of seasonal variations, NFS activities may be grouped into two categories: (i) those competing with agriculture for labour and run parallel to agricultural cycle, and (ii) those that are complementary to agriculture and are taken up during agricultural slack period and linked to agriculture through market demand (Fabella, 1986).

Further, it is argued that NFS can: (i) lower unemployment problem by absorbing growing labour force; (ii) reduce rural-urban migration and thereby contribute in easing urban congestion and lowering pressures on scarce urban infrastructure facilities, (iii) employ women and provide seasonal employment or residual employment for those left out of agriculture and for the poor who cannot find sustenance in agriculture since they are small landholders or landless; (iv) use more appropriate technology, particularly in small scale rural manufacturing and thus generate greater income from available productive inputs; (v) improve household security through diversification; (vi) contribute to national economic growth; (vii) produce commonly consumed goods at lower prices which are mostly demanded by the poor; and (viii) promote a more equitable distribution of income (Lanjouw and Lanjouw: 1995) It is further argued that since redistribution of income through tax-transfer mechanism is politically and administratively difficult in all the developing countries there is a case for focusing on NFS from the point of view of income distribution (Kishor C. Samal: 1997).

Inspite of all these advantages, there is no standard definition of the NFS, either internationally or within India. The sector is too diverse, in terms of activities, unit sizes and geographic dispersal, to allow a neat or precise classification. This is further emphasized by the fact that the sector is usually defined in negative terms as the rural non-farm or non-agricultural sector. Positive terms, such as rural enterprises or rural industries, are inadequate: the former may include agricultural activities; the latter tends to exclude rural services, which in most countries generate more employment than does rural manufacturing.

Various countries have their own specific terms, in China, discussion centres around Township and Village Enterprises (TVEs), an administrative category by ownership; in India, historical causes have often led policymakers to focus on Khadi and Village Industries (KVIs). Yet neither TVEs nor KVIs are coterminous with the rural non-farm or non-agricultural sector, or with rural enterprises or industries. Moreover, the two terms TVEs and KVIs illustrate the very diverse policy perspectives on the NFS that can exist. In China TVEs are at the forefront of the industrial modernization of the state. In India KVIs belong to a largely traditional and partially stagnant sector. (Thomas Fisher, et.al.,: 1997)

However for all official purposes, in India, the National Bank for Agriculture and Rural Development (NABARD) defined NFS, as those enterprises and artisanal activities which could be classified as household, decentralized, tiny and small scale enterprises involved in production/ manufacturing, processing, preserving, storing and marketing of goods and /or engaged in services and agro processing having a bearing on providing employment and incomes to persons residing in rural areas.

In India at present, it is found that NFS has emerged as an alternative to the agricultural sector in absorbing increasing workforce in rural areas. For instance, the percentage of NFS in total rural employment increased from 16.6 percent in 1977-78 to 18.4 percent in 1980, to 21.6 percent in 1993-94 and to 23.8 percent in 1999-2000. The number of workers in NFS increased from 36.1 million in 1977-78 to 44.9 million in 1983 to 62.98 million in 1993-94 to 71.52 million in 1999-2000. Various institutions like National Cooperative Development Corporation, KVIC, State Boards, RBI and commercial banks were promoted or aided NFS activities selectively. Realizing the potential of NFS, the Government of India and the National Bank for Agriculture and Rural Development (NABARD) took number of initiatives for promoting NFS in rural areas. NABARD as the apex institution for rural credit gave a special mandate for development of NFS through credit. Since mid-eighties, a number of policy initiatives such as enhanced rate of refinance, promotional grant assistance for establishment of Technical Monitoring and Evaluation Cells, Training-cum-Production Centres in the banks and conduct of Rural Entrepreneurship Development Programmes, were taken up by NABARD. These efforts have resulted in increasing the refinance support for banks. Though, at the initial stage, the Southern States dominated in availing refinance in recent years, the agriculturally most developed State like Punjab has also availed refinance support for NFS from NABARD.

Banking system also finds this change as new business opportunity. Cooperative Banks, Commercial Banks (CBs) and Regional Rural Banks (RRBs) have availed refinance support from NABARD for financing NFS. (The Institutional Arrangements for Agriculture and Rural Credit in India is given in Chart 1-1).

Statement of the Problem

Institutionalization of rural credit started in India with the enactment of first Cooperative Credit Societies Act of 1904 (K. Ravichandran: 2000). Since then, Primary Agricultural Cooperative Societies (PACS) were organized to provide short term and medium term credit to farmers. Later, a separate agency to provide long term credit to the farmers for redemption of their prior debts and for making permanent improvement on lands was felt, which resulted in the establishment of Land Mortgage Banks (LMB). The first Cooperative LMB was organized in 1920 in Punjab. In Madras Presidency, the first LMB was established in 1929. The LMBs were engaging mainly in the disbursement of loans for redemption of prior debts. After the recommendations of All India Rural Credit Survey Committee (AIRCSC) in 1954, these banks turned towards the issue of loans for productive purposes, instead of, providing loans for redemption of prior debts. Based on the recommendations of AIRCSC Agricultural Refinance Corporation was established which enabled LMBs to expand rapidly and change from being land 'mortgage' banks to land 'development' banks (LDBs).

Between 1956 and 1970, the number of central LDBs increased from 9 to 19, their membership increased from a mere 10,000 to about 10 lakh and the loans outstanding went up from Rs 13 crores to Rs. 507 crores. Over the same period, the number of LDBs grew from 304 to 809, their membership increased from about 3 lakhs to nearly 20 lakhs and outstanding loans went up from Rs. 10 crores to Rs. 367 crores. While the loan business of LDBs increased, the overdues in the structure also increased manifold.

The All India Rural Credit Review Committee (AIRCRC) of 1969 recommended provision of loans from the Reserve Bank of India (RBI) to state governments for contribution to the share capital of LDBs. This recommendation was accepted by the RBI and continued later by the ARDC and NABARD. Another recommendation of the AIRCRC was that Primary Agricultural Credit Societies (PACS) could be used as channels for providing long term credit as agents of the LDBs.

The Long Term Cooperative Credit Structure (LTCCS) was next reviewed by two other Committees, one chaired by Shri K. Madhava Das (Committee on Cooperative Land Development Banks) in 1974 and the second by Dr. R. K. Hazari (Committee on Integration of Cooperation Credit Institutions) in 1975. The Madhava Das Committee, while endorsing diversification of lending operations of the LDBs to cover a broader range of productive activities in agriculture, emphasized the need for greater coordination with the short term structure and the like departments of State Governments. The LT structure had been reviewed by number of other Committees and Commissions in India. They are:

- Committee to Review Arrangements for Institutional Credit for Agriculture and Rural Development (CRAFICARD) (Sivaraman Committee, 1981)
- Agriculture Credit Review Committee (ACRC) (Khusro Committee, 1988)
- Study Group on Deposit Mobilization by ARDBs (Bhandari Committee, 1996)

- Task Force to study the functioning of Cooperative Credit System and Suggest Measures for its Strengthening (Capoor Committee, 2000)
- Expert Committee on Rural Credit (Vyas Committee, 2001)
- Joint Committee on Revitalization Support to Cooperative Credit Structure (Vikhe Patil Committee, 2001).
- Task Force on Revival of Rural Cooperative Credit Institutions (Long Term), (Vaidyanathan Committe, 2006).

The structure of the long term (LT) CCS is distinct from that of the short term (ST) in many ways, even though the LTCCS also has a history dating back to 1920. Although the structure of the LTCCS as a whole is much smaller in size and in business volumes than the Short Term Cooperative Credit Structure (STCCS), its impairment is worse than the latter. We need to keep in mind the following features, which are typical of the LTCCS, before embarking on a more detailed analysis.

The first characteristic of the LTCCS is its limited outreach. Compared to the STCCS, which has over 100,000 retail outlets across the country, commercial and regional rural banks which have a combined network of around 32,000 rural and around 15,000 semi-urban outlets, the LTCCS has only about 2,500 retail outlets. In the years following bank nationalization and the multi agency approach to rural credit, the LTCCS lost its position as the dominant source for long-term credit. The limited outreach of the LTCCS implies that although an LTCCS outlet theoretically covers a large area, its ability to extend financial support to the population resident therein is questionable.

The second important feature of the LTCCS is the limited range of products and services offered by it. In most cases, the LTCCS offers only long term loans. However, in recent years, some of them have started providing, in a very limited way, crop loans and gold loans. It is obvious that with such a limited range of credit products and almost no other financial services, the LTCCS are ill-equipped to compete with commercial banks, Regional Rural Banks (RRBs) and even the STCCS. The large service area per outlet means that borrowers are scattered over a large geographical area. This results in infrequent interactions among members, which makes it difficult for these institutions, especially in the unitary structure, to function effectively as genuine cooperatives.

Scattered lending over a large geographical area, restricted to only long term loans which are needed by farmers rather infrequently, results in infrequent contact with borrowers and makes monitoring of loan usage less effective and more costly. These traits have adverse implications on prompt recovery of loans. The exclusivity in dealing with only long term loans also creates a pressure in terms of resource mobilization and management of liabilities. Although, State Cooperative Agriculture and Rural Development Banks (SCARDBs) accept term deposits, these are neither at the primary level, nor from the borrower members. In other words there should be a counter-balancing mechanism within the cooperative that drives prudent fund management.

These problems are compounded by the structural diversity in the LTCCS across states. Unlike the STCCS, which has a federal structure in the entire country even if it has three tiers in some states and two in others, the LT structure does not have a common design. This diversity makes comparing data across states, regions and even across the designs themselves difficult. The country has four different types of structures under the LTCCS at present, described in Chart 1.1. The Structure of Long Term (LT) is not uniform across the State. Federal, Unitary mixed and integrated structures exist at present (Appendices Chart-1). There were 768 Primary Cooperative Agriculture and Rural Development Banks (PCARDBs) functioning at primary level. There were 20 SCARDBs functioning at State level. In Tamilnadu the State Cooperative Agriculture and Rural Development Bank is functioning with 181 PCARDBs as its members. In this context, it becomes necessary to analyze: whether policies and procedures followed for disbursing NFS loans suit the needs of the users? Whether the NFS loans helped in the generation of employment and poverty reduction in rural areas? What is the socio-economic profile of NFS loan borrowers? These and other such questions should be addressed through micro level studies, so as to enable institutions as well as policy makers to tune the efforts of the PCARDBs towards the achievement of their objectives. Hence the present study is undertaken to study the performance of PCARDBs two districts in Tamil Nadu namely Dindugal and Nagapattinam districts regarding their role in developing NFS.

Review of Literature

The potential of NFS in solving the twin problems viz., unemployment and poverty attracted many social scientists. A number of studies have been conducted on different aspects of NFS during recent past. The major issues dealt by these studies were pattern of NFS, NFS and income generation, labour market and linkages between agriculture and NFS. The available studies are reviewed here under.

Several studies pointed out the fact that the NFS does not consist of a homogeneous set of activities in terms of income and productivity levels. Some studies suggested that the NFS consists of two sub-sectors. Sector one are enterprises run on a more or less stable basis with an eye on surplus generation and growth, hiring labour and with a certain degree of technical sophistication. Sector two consists of products or activities which are often seasonal, run solely with the help of unpaid family labour, using primitive technology and catering mostly to the local market. According to them the differences in the two sub-sectors are discernible in terms of capital use and production relations rather than product categories. A third category of 'wage-paid' employment sector characterized by low earnings and atomized markets with respect to labour supply is also distinguished.

A study conducted by Chauhan S.P. (1994) found that "due to introduction of labour saving technology, the employment prospects of people, particularly the landless agricultural workers, had been reduced in agriculture".

"A Study on Rural Non-Agricultural Employment in Kerala", conducted by Mridul Eapen (1994), found "a rather paradoxical situation wherein the employment structure in rural areas did not show any significant overall improvement but rural prosperity had increased, and also among casual workers".

Lanjouw and Peter Lanjouw (1995) in their study on NFS and Employment found that in most countries projects to support small-scale and rural enterprise continue to be undertaken in a general policy environment which was biased against them.

A study conducted by Satyendra P. Gupta (1996) revealed that income from Non-Farm Employment (NFE) was also important to improve economic conditions of the farmers.

Jeemol Unni (1996) through his study on Diversification of Economic Activities and Non-Agricultural Employment in Rural Gujarat found that the chances of diversification into more than one economic activity were higher among agricultural households and individual agricultural workers. Access to land facilitates this process. Seasonality in agriculture, uncertainty and risks in production also create a greater need to diversify. In far away and less developed villages diversification was likely to be due to low and uncertain incomes from one economic activity.

Kishore C. Samal (1997) found that the level and growth of NFS differ from region to region. The income from NFS as a percentage of total household income has increased rapidly in industrially developed region. While analyzing the features and determinants of NFS in Orissa it was concluded that equal distribution of land and rural assets including common property resources and water for irrigation and NFS activities were positively related. However whether inequality in distribution of income increases or decreases due to participation in NFS activities was not easy to say. It is necessary to recognize the dichotomy in the rural non-farm sector when analyzing its linkages with the farm sector because the growth pattern will be different in the various sub-sectors. According to Samal the rural non-farm consisted of formal and informal sub-sectors. The informal sector is further subdivided into the modern and traditional sectors. The latter consisting of caste based artisan and service workers, of which particularly the former is expected to be adversely affected by agricultural development.

Parthasarathy G. Shameem and B. Sambi Reddy (1998) concluded in their study that policy measures were needed to translate output into employment by promoting larger investment in land, both public and private, particularly by small farmers.

A study conducted by Nagaiya D. (1999) on NFS in Andhra Pradesh—found that States which had shown relatively fast growth in employment in the NFS were generally the ones which also recorded a relatively better growth in agriculture. Thus, development of NFS, though largely dependent on agriculture growth, seems to be a process characterized by simultaneous growth in several sectors such as transport, trade, construction and of course manufacturing.

Bhagirathi Panda (1999) found that in Arunachal Pradesh the share of Rural Non Farming Employment (RNFE) had continuously increased and that of Rural Farming Employment (RFE) has continuously decreased. The rate of increase had been higher than the annual growth rate of rural population.

Studies conducted on Non-Farm Rural Livelihoods by Ann Gordon (1999), strongly supported that a vibrant agricultural sector created demand for consumption goods (and employment) in the NFS. Policies which promoted agricultural sector also promote NFS.

Sudhakar Reddy, E. (2000) opined that the programme for rural non-farm employment as distinguished from the programme for industrialization requires a separate strategy in terms of its procedures and provisions, method of implementation and administration. If not all, a few of these need a clear-cut specification. The political economy of these schemes was the most important matter. NF Sector was more broad based compared to rural industrialization. This needs to be built into the programme for NFS.

Mahender Dev (2001) found that non-farm employment expands due to push and pull factors like study income, regular work and fixed timing.

Ramachandraiah, G. (2002) while studying the Institutions and Infrastructural impediments in Rural industrialization in Dindugal District found that since the enterprises were started on the basis of product and good resource base, their success rate was found to be very high as 90 percent of the enterprises were working very well and only 10 percent had small problems. However, they were also slowly becoming successful.

A study conducted by R. Ravindra Pirabu and C. Thangamuthu (2003) brings out a revealing trend: the SC households had the prospect of improving their economic standards by migrating to (or daily commuting to) the urban areas and getting better paid jobs in NFE. Some types of NFE which the SC labour could get access to in the urban areas, might not be available, or accessible to the Scheduled Castes in their villages, given the social hierarchy and labour market imperfections arising out of the caste system.

A study by Tiago Wandschneider (2003) found that the fortunes of the two sectors farm and non farm were intimately intertwined.

A study conducted by NABARD Kerala Regional Office (2004), Non-Farm sector plays a vital role in the uplift of the rural poor at the grass root level. This sector has the ability to generate high income and employment with small investments.

Rana Bijoy Deb (2004) opined that inspite of various constraints, which stand on their way in utilizing plant capacities, the rural units were able to generate more employment with low involvement of capital as compared to their urban counterparts. The above studies clearly correlated the growth or pattern of NFS with rural livelihoods particularly, employment and income generation. Other important input which induces the growth of NFS in credit. Very limited studies have been conducted on this.

NABARD (2005) conducted Expert Evaluation Study on NFS in Andra Pradesh. The study found that credit flow to NFS had increased over time. Main reasons for default among units were: insufficient and irregular orders (fashion technology), weaning away of the members from the group by private traders (coir mat), non-utilization of the machines (coir rope). Also some studies found that a positive link between literacy levels and number of non-farm enterprises in the villages seems to be the result of increased awareness and aspirations among literates about new and better modes of livelihoods. Manufacturing activities are seen as engines of growth due to their significant positive spread effects on other activities and resources. In non-farm sector as well, these activities have an important role to play.

There are a number of studies conducted on the functioning of long term credit structure. Majority of the studies have been on the problem of overdue and recovery.

It was found that the causes for overdue were natural calamities, low income (Bhuanandran, P.: 1992) (Anandagopal D. Kulandaiswamy, V.: 1989 and Veerakumaran, G.: 1995) willful default and misutilisation (Jaya Anand, S.: 1995). Some studies on cost of recovery found that cost of recovery was observed to be strongly correlated with the recovery performance of the banks and more than 50 percent of recovery cost was accounted to salary and daily allowance (Tiwary, S.N.:1991) (Rao, D.S.P. 1992 and Joy Joseph Puthussery: 1998).

It shows that overdue had been a major problem for PCARDBs over the period. The entry of PCARDBs in NFS activities attracted very poor response from research world. Boothalingam M. (1995), while studying NFS and cooperatives found that by and large the schemes for which loans were given increased the income rather than employment potential.

It shows that very few studies are available on the role of cooperatives in promoting NFS. The present study attempts to fill up this research gap by studying the role of PCARDBs in NFS at micro level.

Objectives of the Study

The present study has the following objectives:

1. to study the economic profile of sample banks,
2. to analyze the policies, procedures and their performance relating to NFS in the selected bank,
3. to examine the role of NFS in income, employment generation and poverty reduction in rural areas and
4. to suggest suitable measures for the effective operation of Non-Farm sector loans.

Hypotheses

The hypotheses for the study are:

1. NFS helped in income generation in rural areas.
2. NFS generated employment opportunities in rural areas.

Definition of Concepts and Terms

Age

This is the number of years completed by the respondent on the date of interview.

Ancillary Industry

An industrial undertaking which is engaged in the manufacture of parts, components, sub-assemblies, tooling or intermediates or rendering services and which supplies atleast 50 percent of its production or services to one or more other industrial undertakings and whose investment in plant and machinery does not exceed Rs. 1 crore.

Artisan

Rural craftsmen possessing manual skill in operation of small tools and machines, either in self-employment or working for another artisan for earning one's livelihood.

Borrowings

It is the total amount borrowed by a respondent through all available sources expressed in Rs. 10,000 (here one unit is Rs. 10,000).

Contact with Change Agents

It is the frequency of contacts which the respondents had with the change agents per month.

Cottage Industry

Industries in which fixed capital does not exceed Rs. 25,000 (some States have revised it upto Rs.60,000) and the number of persons employed is less than 9.

Craftsman (Handicraftsman)

Craftsman producing articles by skill of the hand and a special vocation acquired over a period. A handicraft article to be distinct from rural craft must undergo atleast one operation/process involving skill of hand. They cover artistic/utilitarian handicrafts.

Decentralized Sector

A sector of economy in which articles of common / local use are produced locally, utilizing by and large, locally available natural resources and human skills.

Duration of Membership

It is the total number of years from the date of membership in the cooperative society till date.

Education

Level of education is classified into five categories:

a. No Formal Education—not studied in any school.
b. Primary—studied from first standard to fifth standard.
c. Secondary—studied from sixth standard to tenth standard (SSLC).

d. Higher Secondary—studied upto Twelfth standard (Plus two after SSLC).

e. Degree—three years degree course in arts and science colleges and

f. Professional Degree—degrees obtained in medicine, engineering etc.,

Employment Generation

It is the number of man-days generated by the respondents by investing the loan amounts on various NFS activities. In this study eight hours of work is taken as one manday.

Family Size

It is the number of members living under one roof and cooking in the same kitchen.

Household Industry

Cottage industry in which at least one member of the family is actively engaged in production activity.

Income Generated

It is the total income obtained through various investments made with the help of borrowed amount on various NFS activities.

Industry

Any productive activity involving collection, processing, preservation, manufacturing, repairing, addition, alteration, servicing, etc., covering all types of secondary activities are referred here as industry.

Investments

It is the total amount invested by the respondent on various NFS activities exp essed in Rs.10,000 (here one unit is Rs.10,000).

Mass-media Exposure

It is the aggregate score computed on the basis of scores given for each one of the item in the mass media.

Non Performing Assets

Non Performing Assets is an indicator of how much of the advances do not generate income for the bank.

Number of Investments

It is the total number of investments made by the respondents on various NFS activities.

Rural Area

Area comprised in any village irrespective of population and also in any town, where the population does not exceed 50, 000.

Rural Industry

An activity using, predominantly manpower situated in rural areas and local resources are used to transform inputs into finished goods.

Non-Farm Sector (NFS)

NFS is defined as those enterprises and artisanal activities which could be classified as household, decentralized, tiny and small scale enterprises involved in production/ manufacturing, processing, preserving, storing and marketing of goods and /or engaged in services and agro processing having a bearing on providing employment and income to persons residing in rural areas.

Service Industry

Inclusion of "Service" within the industry has widened the coverage of secondary sector (dry cleaning, medical clinics, beauty parlours also included) units with investment in plant & machinery upto Rs.2 lakh and located in areas upto 5 lakh population.

Sex

This is a binary variable with one for male and zero for female.

Small Scale Industry

An industrial undertaking in which, the investment in plant & machinery does not exceed Rs.1 crore.

Tiny Sector Unit

Any industrial concern in which, the investment in plant and machinery does not exceed Rs.25 lakhs.

Unorganized Units/Informal Sector

Units which are not registered/foot loose units

Village Industry

Khadi and Village Industrial Units located in areas upto 20,000 population and in which the capital investment is less than Rs. 50,000 per year per person employed.

Methodology

Survey Method was adopted for the study. Empirical analysis of sample units was done to understand the operational issues and sectoral distribution of NFS finance provided by PCARDBs. Detailed schedule were prepared and administered to collect data relating to the problem. Suitable statistical tools were used to analyze the data and derive conclusions.

Sampling

For the purpose of the study a three stage sampling procedure was adopted.

First Stage

In the first stage two districts were selected; one agriculturally developed and one agriculturally under developed district i.e., Dindugal and Nagapattinam (Map 1and 2).

Second Stage

In, the second stage, all the nine PCARDBs functioning in these two districts (Six in Dindugal district and Three in Nagapattinam district) were selected for the study.

Third Stage

There were 41,562 members in Dindugal district (in all nine PCARDBs put together) and 31,434 members in Nagapattinam district (in all three PCARDBs put together). Out of them totally there were only 6,140 NFS beneficiaries in both the districts put together. Hence in the next stage 10 percent of the NFS beneficiaries were selected using stratified simple random sampling method. The sample size in Dindugal district is 352 and in Nagapattinam district 262. Therefore the sample size is 614.

Collection of Data

A detailed interview schedule for the PCARDBs was prepared and administrated. It was structured with various questions like general information related to NFS, loan issued to members, overdue outstanding, recovery of loan – purpose wise, and position of NPA etc. The interview schedule was pre-tested and the questions were structured to facilitate speedy completion of needed data / information. Two types of schedules were used: (i) one for sample PCARDBs and (ii) members. The interview schedule was used for the collection of data regarding organizational structure, loan policies and procedures and the perception of the officials towards NFS loans. Data relating to Membership, Share capital, Reserve funds, Borrowings, Deposits, were also collected.

Another interview schedule was constructed for eliciting information from members regarding their sex, age, education, family size, mass media exposure, contact with change agents, duration of membership, borrowings and investments, so as to enable the researcher to test hypothesis framed.

Framework of Analysis

Statistical tools like correlation analysis, linear regression, path analysis, the mean and standard deviation were used. These techniques are intended to study the changes in the selected variables and the interaction of the variables with dependant variable. The independent variables are sex, age, education, family size, exposure to mass media, contact with change agents, membership, borrowings and investments. The dependent variables are employment and income (Box-1).

Box-1
Variables

*Dependent variable**	*Independent variable**
1. Employment	Demographic: Sex, Age
2. Income	Social: Education, Family size, Exposure to mass media, contact with change Agents, Membership.
	Economic: Borrowings and Investment.

* A detailed explanation is given in the Chapter 4.

Period of Study

The study covered a period of 5 years. (i.e. from 2001–2002, to 2005 – 2006).

Limitations of the Study

The present study is not far from limitations. PCARDBs have identified NFS as a business opportunity. Though the issue of loans to NFS started as early as 1990s, still focused attention is lacking, which is evident from the fact that classified data with regard to NFS loan operation at PCARDBs as well as at SCARDBs level are not readily available; therefore the data regarding certain indicators were not available for the study period. However, due care has been taken to present the data for the study period i.e., 2001-02 to 2005-06. Hence, NF Sector wise borrowers could not be selected as sample for the study. Further, the study is focused primarily on only two selected districts of Tamilnadu, its limitations are acknowledged. However, this has not affected the purpose of the present study and its logical presentation.

Chapter Scheme

Based on the objectives of the study, the report of the thesis is presented in the following five chapters.

1. The first chapter deals with the Design and Execution of the Study.
2. The second chapter presents the Environmental and Economic Profile of the sample PCARDBs.
3. The third chapter analyses the Business Policies and Performance of PCARDBs with special reference to Non Farm Sector loans
4. The fourth chapter analyses the role of NFS in employment generation and poverty reduction.
5. The fifth chapter presents the Findings, Conclusion and Suggestions of the study.

Chart – 1.1

Institutional Arrangements for Agriculture and Rural Credit in India

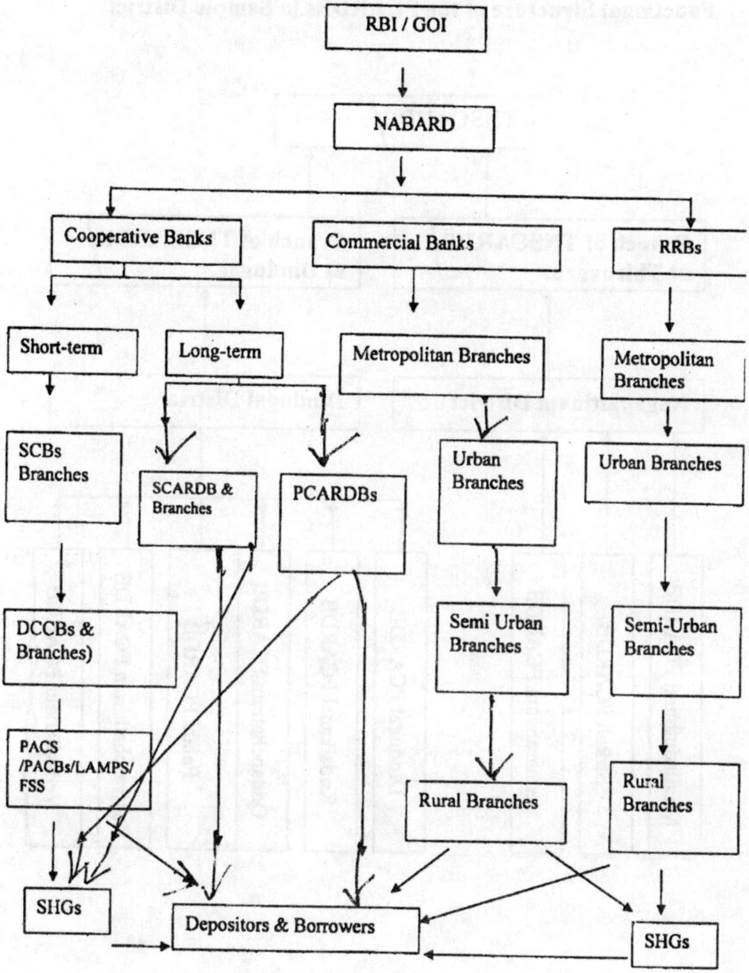

Chart 1.2

Functional Structure of the PCARDBs in Sample District

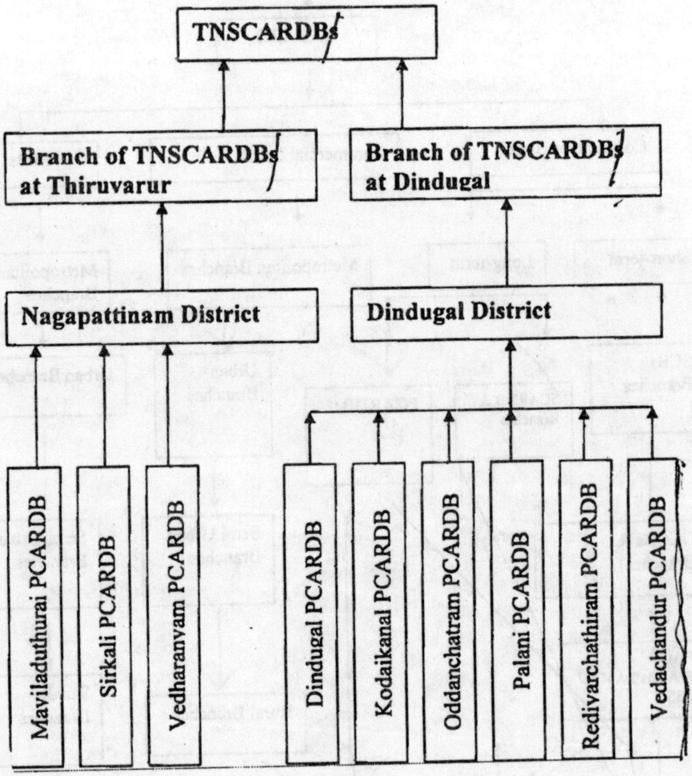

2

Economic Profile of the Sample PCARDBs

Small, Tiny and Cottage Industries have contributed in a significant way for the development of rural areas in Tamilnadu by providing employment and income to a large section of population. Non Farm Sector in the State is dominated by the activities like power loom, handloom, agro based industries, leather based activities, general engineering, plastic based industries, gem cutting, electric and electronic industry, chemical industry, handicraft, hotel and restaurants, etc. NFS in the State registered 2.53 per cent annual growth during last decade and generated around one fifth of total employment generated in rural area. The State accounted for around 70 per cent of the total leather tanning capacity in the country and contributed 31 per cent of cotton yarn production by the country. More than 60 per cent of power driven in the country was also produced in the State.

Role of NFS in the State still continues to be high as the capacity of agricultural sector to absorb growing population is shrinking in the wake of farm mechanization and shifting of cropping pattern in favour of labour saving crops. Development of NFS has the advantage like use of locally available inputs, diversified product mix, enabling market available at locally, involve low level of technology and capital, environmental friendly, improve income level of farmers by way of value addition etc. Government of Tamilnadu facilitate at the NFS for enhancing growth and dynamism and also to improve the quality of its products. For better understanding of this sector a brief analysis is made here under on the physical and infrastructural features of Tamilnadu and the sample districts. On these backgrounds the functioning of PCARDBs in sample districts is made hereunder.

Physical Features

Tamil Nadu, the southern most State of India, is located in North Latitude between 80°5′ and 13°35′, and East Longitude between 76°15′ and 80°20′. The State is bounded by Kerala on the West, Andhra Pradesh and Karnataka on the North, Bay of Bengal on the East and Indian Ocean in the South. Point Calimere is at the eastern tip and Mudumalai Sanctuary is at the western tip of the State. Pulicat Lake and Cape Comorin are the northern and southern extremes of the State. For administrative convenience, the State is divided into 29 districts including state capital Chennai and further into 201 taluks.

Tamil Nadu occupies 4 per cent of India's geographical area but possesses only 3 per cent of the water resources of India. The total geographical area of the State is 12.99 million ha. Entire Eastern part of the State has coastal line having a length of 992 km. Climate in the State is mainly tropical and temperature ranges between 43°C and 18°C. State receives moderate rainfall and the major share of which (around 48 per cent) is received through North East monsoon during the month of October–December. Major rivers in the State are Cauvery, Vaigai, Tamiraparani, Palar, Ponniar and Vellar.

As per Agro Climatic Regional Planning by Planning Commission of India, districts in the State falls under three Agro-climatic zones viz., *(i)* Southern Plateau & Hills (Zone-X) Dharmapuri, Salem, Erode, Coimbatore, Madurai, Theni,

Dindugal, Trichy, Karur, Perembalore districts, *(ii)* East Coast Plains and Hills, (Zone-XI) Chennai, Kancheepuram, Tiruvallur, Vellore, Cuddalore, Villupuram, Tiruvannamalai, Thanjavur, Tiruvarur, Nagapattinam, Podukkottai, Ramnad, Toothukudi, Sivaganga, Virudhunagar and Tirunelveli; and, *(iii)* West Coast & Hills, (Zone-XII) Kanyakumari and Nilgiris districts. Soil in the State mainly belongs to the category of red loamy, red sandy, black soil, deltaic alluvium and coastal alluvium. Forest occupies 16.42 per cent of the total geographical area of the State as against 22.6 per cent for country.

Dindugal district was formed on 15 September 1985 by carving out of Madurai district. The District has 3 Revenue Divisions (Dindugal, Palani, Kodaikkanal), 7 taluks, 14 development blocks, 39 firkas and 359 revenue villages covering a geographical area of 6266.64 sq. km. This district covers about 4.81 percent of the geographical area of the State. It has a population of 19.23 lakh (2001 census) with predominantly rural population (12.47 lakh or 65 percent of total population). The population of the district constitutes 3.08 percent of the state's population. The district is located between 10°05" and 10°09" North latitudes and 77°30" and 78°20" East longitudes. It is bounded by Erode, Karur, Coimbatore and Thiruchirapalli districts in the North, by Sivagangai and Thiruchirapalli districts in the East, by Madurai and Theni districts in the South and by Coimbatore and Theni districts and Kerala State in the West. The district receives an average annual rainfall of 836 mm with the major portion of the precipitation being received from the north eastern monsoons.

The district has extensive hilly areas with undulating plains. All along the western fringes of the district lie the Palani Hill ranges of the Western Ghats ranging in height from 1000 to 2700 meters MSL. The upper hills comprise of peaks like Perumalmalai and Vandarverimalai and are home to the beautiful, serene, salubrious hill station, Kodaikkanal. The lower plains are made up of hills like Thandikudi and Virupatchi. On the eastern fringes a large number of isolated hill ranges like Sirumalai, Alagarmalai,

Karandamalai, Kodangimalai, Rangamalai, Pillayarnatham, Natham and Ayyalur are found. The rest of the district is characterized by an undulating plain covered mostly (85 percent) by red soil. Black earth covers the rest of the plains.

A few seasonal rivers like, tributaries of the Vaigai, Amaravathi, Kodaganar, Kuthiraiyar, Manjalar, Palar, Porandalar, Parappalar, Santhanavardhini, Shanmuganathi, Varathamanathi flow through the district. There are seven small dams in the district, viz., Varathamanathi, Palar-Porundalar, Kuthiraiyar, Parappalar, Kamarajar and Mavur with a total water storage capacity of 2787.28 million cft and total canal length of 114.79 km. The gross irrigated area is 99981 ha, which is about 37.82 percent of the total cropped area of 264367 ha. Out of the 14 blocks in the district, only one block viz., Kodaikanal has been classified as 'safe' for groundwater exploitation as per the latest groundwater assessment by the State Ground Water Department. Though the district received a rainfall of 1124mm during 2004-05, it is drought prone and has received less than average rainfall during the previous two years. Very small land holdings of less than one ha account for 67 percent of the total holdings but constitute only 23 percent area of land holdings.

In the case of Nagapattinam district (originally named as Nagai Quaid-e-Milleth District) was formed by carving out certain portions of the erstwhile Thanjavur District. Again in January 1997, the district was reorganized into Nagapattinam District with 11 blocks, is bounded by Cuddalore District in the North, Thiruvarur District in the West, Palk Strait in the South and Bay of Bengal in the East. The district is geographically not contiguous, with Karaikal (UTP) located between the Mayiladuthural division in the north and Nagapattinam division in the south. Nagapattinam is a predominantly agricultural district with the net sown area constituting nearly 53 per cent of the total geographical area as against only 39 per cent for the state as a whole. Major area is irrigated by well developed canal irrigation system with net irrigated area constituting 83 per cent of net sown area as against 51.74 per cent for the State. However, water supply is dependent upon the availability of water in the river Cauvery which drains into Bay of Bengal through vast net work of canals traversing the district.

Demographic Features

According to 2001 census, Tamil Nadu has a population of 62.11 million and is the sixth most populous State in the country. The decadal growth rate in population (1991-2001) is 11.19 per cent as against 21.34 per cent recorded for the country. Birth rate in the State declined from 31.4 in 1971 to 19.3 in 2000. Death rate has declined from 14.4 to 9.9 between 1971 and 2000. Tamilnadu is classified as one of the most urbanized States in the country with 42 per cent of its population living in urban areas.

Dindugal district, it covers the geographical area of 6266.64 Sq. Km with a population of 19.23 lakh (2001 census). The population is predominantly rural comprising of 65 percent (12.47 lakhs) as against 55.9 percent for the state.

Nagapattinam district accounts for 2.08 percent of the geographical area with a population comprising of 2.39 percent of the State. The population is predominantly rural comprising of 77.8 percent as against 55.9 percent for the State.

Socio-Economic Features

Agriculture is the mainstay of the rural economy of Tamil Nadu. It provides livelihood to 65 per cent of the State's population and contributes 62 per cent of employment generated in the State. This sector contributes on an average 20 per cent to the State's Net Domestic Product. Being the dominant sector, the improvement or changes in the State output depends upon the output of agriculture. Thus, there are strong links between agriculture and overall economic growth of the State. The agricultural policy of the State aims at an ever-green revolution by improving productivity in dry land agriculture, value addition to agricultural products, watershed and wasteland development, pest and water management.

The extent of Gross State Domestic Product is an important index of State economic growth. It is envisaged to have a growth rate of 8 per cent during the Tenth Five Year Plan period. The economy of the State has undergone transformation over the last few decades. The share of Primary Sector which was 53.27 per cent during 1950-51 has declined to 16.65 per cent in 2001-02. On the other hand, the share of secondary and tertiary Sectors has increased from 13.72 per cent and 33 per cent respectively in 1950-51 to 34.04 per cent and 49.3 per cent in 2001-02. The per capita income of the State was Rs. 19889 (at current prices) during 2000-01 and ranks fourth in the country in terms of per capita income. As per the composite index of infrastructure development constructed by Centre for Monitoring Indian Economy, Tamil Nadu was the third best in the country.

In Dindugal district agriculture and animal husbandry are the predominant economic activities. Industry, business and commerce are also other important activities prevalent in the district. Leather tanning, cotton spinning and cement industries are the major industries of the district. Quite a few small scale engineering and allied industries function in the district. Food processing and chemical industries have also come up in recent times. The traditional industry for which the district is known for the lock and Iron Safe manufacturing industry where the manual processes still continue. A small town in the district, Chinnalapatti is famous for its handloom cotton and synthetic (art silk) sungudi sarees. Dindugal has a flourishing trade in onions, groundnut and tobacco. A large fruit and vegetable market at Oddanchatram serves not only the state but also the neighbouring states as well. The district has an important pilgrimage centre, Palani, where the famous Bala Dandayudhapani temple is situated. Kodaikkanal, a popular hill resort of South India, is also located in the district. These two places have a flourishing tourism industry. The district also has many service sector industries.

A wide range of fruit, flower and vegetable crops are grown in the district in addition to agricultural crops like paddy, cholam, cumbu, cotton, tobacco, groundnut, pulses and oilseeds. Coconut is one of the major plantation crops grown in the plains. Coffee, pepper, lemon, jackfruit, cardamom and other spices, subtropical fruits, flowers and vegetables are grown in the hilly areas of the district. Some of the major industries in district are handloom weaving, lock and safe manufacturing in the traditional sector and cotton/polyester spinning, leather tanning, food processing like flour, vermicelli manufacturing industries. A few modern agro processing industries have been established in the medium and small scale sectors.

Dindugal is one of the very few districts which have two distinct agro climatic zones, viz., semi arid tropical climate in the plains and subtropical climate in the hills of Western Ghats mainly in Kodaikkanal block.

There is good scope for value addition by way of processing a large variety of horticultural produce of the district. A major portion of the produce is sold in fresh form. The Agro Processing Complex at Pallapatti can be popularized to give a fillip to the activity. Quite a few flower (chiefly jasmine) perfume extraction plants have come up recently in and around Nilakottai where large area is under cultivation of jasmine (malligai, mullai, pitchi). Kodaikanal block offers scope for geranium oil extraction and cut flowers. The medicinal plants grown in the district are *Gloriosa superba,* Aloe vera, *Aswagandha (Withania somnifera),* etc. The extracts of aromatic plants have an excellent potential for export in addition to good domestic demand.

In Nagapattinam district agriculture, dairying, fishing, goat rearing and shrimp farming are the principal occupations under the primary sector. Pottery, cane works, mat weaving, palm products and handicrafts coir rope making, etc. under Cottage and Village Industries Sector and ready-made garments, furniture works etc. under the Small Scale Industries (SSI) sector are some of the major activities pursued. Tourism is gaining importance in the district.

This district lies in the tail end region of Cauvery delta. Fisheries are next only to agriculture in terms of its contribution to the economy and livelihood for the people. With a long coastal line of 188 km, the district offers very good scope for development of fisheries. The district contributes 12.39 per cent of marine fish produced in the State. Almost 40 per cent of the potential of the State for coastal shrimp farming is located in the district. The brackish water shrimp culture units have to be properly regularized for development in this region to take advantage of the long coastline. Suitability of sea-bass has also been tested at the Rajiv Gandhi Centre for Aqua-culture, Thirumullaivasal and efforts are on to commercialize sea bass culture in coastal areas. The district is one of the leading districts in terms of marine fish production and large number of shrimp farms are located along its along coastline. Post harvest techniques in fisheries sector are being propagated by Department of Fisheries and other agencies.

Desilting of canals was taken up in a big way during the past by the State Government which would improve the efficiency of irrigation systems in the district. Recently, farm ponds are being constructed which will help in rain water harvesting for recycling as well as for irrigation. Being a delta district, the entire rainwater is lost as runoff into the sea. Rain water harvesting structures like farm ponds are advocated in the district for recharging groundwater and reducing the salinity of groundwater due to ingression of sea water. Concerted efforts are needed for developing entrepreneurship for taking up industrial ventures in the district.

The district was worst affected by the Tsunami tidal waves on 26 December 2004 with maximum loss of life and property. The entire fishery infrastructure was devastated and the coastal fisher folk affected. After the relief phase, the process of rehabilitation has commenced with major thrust on rebuilding the livelihood of the coastal communities and construction of permanent shelters on public-private partnership basis in addition to voluntary action. The fishing harbours at Nagapattinam, Pazhayar and Kodiakarai are in the process of rebuilding along with other major fish landing centers with support from agencies like Asian Development Bank. Steel boats are being introduced in the place of damaged wooden fishing vessels. The Agriculture/ Horticulture lands affected by the salinity of the tidal waves are being reclaimed with assistance from the Government and Non Governmental Organisations (NGOs).

The mineral resources in the form of crude oil and natural gas are available in the district. The important major minerals available in Nagapattinam District are Crude Oil, Natural Gas, Silica Sand, Lime shell, Heavy Mineral sand (Garnet, Iluminite, Rutile Zircon, Monozite). Silica sand available in the Vedaranyam coast is best suited for manufacturing sodium silicate. Annually 20000 tonnes of silica sand is exploited mainly by 10 sodium silicate units located in Karaikal region. Salt is one of main mineral resources in the district with salt production in the coastal area of Vedaranyam.

The district is having age-old maritime relationship with the countries of South East Asia especially Singapore and Malaysia. The port which was damaged during recent Tsunami is being renovated. The district has an extensive network of Commercial Banks and cooperative institutions. The district has good scope for development of allied sectors especially inland and coastal aquaculture, dairy and goat rearing. The district is known for pilgrim centers like Vellanganni and Nagore, Navagraha temples apart from a good number of temples built during the Chola regime. There is a good scope for developing tourism related investments in the district, as there are places of historic importance like Tharangambadi, Poompuhar, Vedaranyam and Kodikarai.

Infrastructure

Tamil Nadu has a rail network of 4181 km which accounted for 6.36 per cent of the total length in the country. Electrified network accounted for 21.46 per cent of the total route length. The State has one of the best road networks in the country with 3865 km of Highways, 7136 km of State Highways, 7408 km of Major District Roads and 40853 km of other District Roads. The State has four domestic ports viz., Chennai, Ennore and Toothukudi. The State has four domestic air ports viz., Chennai, Coimbatore, Trichy and Madurai and one International airport at Chennai. More than 10 per cent of total air passengers and air cargo in the country are handled by the airports in the State. The State has a sound network of communication. There are 8362 post offices, 3805 P&T offices and 108 Telegraph offices.

Dindugal district has a fairly good network of bank branches. There are 23 Commercial Banks which operate with their 138 branches in the district. The short term co-operative structure, viz, the Dindugal District Central Co-operative Bank Ltd (DDCCB) has a network of 29 branches as well as 193 affiliated Primary Agricultural Credit Societies (PACS). The long term co-operative structure operates through 6 PCARDBs (Map-1). Pandyan Grama Bank operates in the district with 02 branches.

Nagapatinam district has a network 17 branches of CBs and 3 PCARDBs (Map-2). These CBs have 53 branches in rural area and 41 branches in semi urban area. The Kumbakonam Central Cooperative Bank (KCCB) extends its area of operation in Nagapattinam district also by having 10 branches and 112 Primary Agriculture Cooperative Banks (PACBs).

To generate employment opportunities in rural areas and to improve rural economy, the Government of Tamilnadu have announced a Scheme called "New Anna Marumalarchi Thittam" to promote agro-based food processing industries with minimum capital investment of Rs. 1 Crore and above in each of the 385 blocks of the state utilizing the locally available agricultural produces. Each block can have a maximum of 4 units, each with a minimum capital of Rs. 25 lakh to satisfy Rs. 1.00 Crore norm of capital investment for each block. The scheme is implemented through District Industries Centre (DIC). The special packages and incentive to each project are 15 percent capital investment subsidy on plant and machinery, 5 percent additional capital investment subsidy for employment of women workforce, 15 percent generator subsidy on the cost of generator, Low Tension Power Tariff subsidy at the rate of 30 percent for the first year, 20 percent for the second year and 10 percent for the third year. The escort support in the preparation of project reports, access to funding, obtaining statutory clearances and power connection for the projects are provided by the District Collector and General Manager, DIC. With these backgrounds the functioning of LT structure both at national level and state level is presented hereunder.

Functioning of LT Structure at National Level

At all India level the structure of long term credit is not uniform. Federal, unitary, mixed and integrated structure exist at present (refer Fig. 1.2), The National federation of State Agriculture and Rural Development Bank is functioning at Mumbai. The main function of this federation is advocacy. At the State level, there are 20 State level federations of ARDBs functioning across the country. The number is small compared to number of States in India. Because in some States DCCBs look after the functions of federation, while in other cases one State federation covers more than one State, especially in the case of North Eastern States. The State level federation has branches, which are generally located at District head quarters. This arrangement has been made to facilitate and integrate the functioning of PCARDBs at primary level.

Table 2.1

Performance of SCARDBs at National Level

(Rs. in Crore)

	2000-2001	*2001-2002*	*2002-2003*	*2003-2004*	*2004-2005*
Number	20	20	20	20	20
Branches	663	887 (33.78)	858 (-3.26)	766 (-10.72)	791 (3.26)
Owned funds	2386	2484 (4.10)	2891 (16.38)	2977 (2.97)	3549 (19.21)

Deposits	535	572 (6.91)	545 (-4.72)	587 (7.70)	608 (3.57)
Borrowings	13431	14845 (10.52)	15910 (7.17)	16900 (6.22)	17114 (1.26)
Loan Issued	2586	2747 (6.22)	2964 (7.89)	2837 (-4.28)	3292 (16.03)
Loan outstanding	11400	14147 (24.09)	15385 (8.75)	16224 (5.45)	17390 (7.18)

Source : Compiled from Annual Reports of NABARD for various years.
Note: Figures in Parenthesis shows the percentage of change.

As such there were 663 branches of SCARDBs functioning in our country during the year 2000–01. This has increased to 887 branches in 2001–02 and came down to 791 in 2004–05. The reduction in number of branches was due to reorganization of States.

In the case of owned funds, it was found that in the year 2000–01, the total owned fund owned by these federations was Rs. 2386 crores. This has increased over the years and stood at Rs. 3549 crores in 2004–05. As discussed hereunder, these banks are not concentrating on deposit mobilization which is evident from the fact that the total deposit mobilized was Rs. 535 crores in 2000 – 01. This has grown over the years and stood at Rs. 608 crores in 2004–05. Due to Government waiving policies across the country, the total loan issued by the structure also affected severely.

Performance of PCARDBs at National Level

The Primary Cooperative Agriculture and Rural Development Banks are at the bottom level of loan distribution to members. They collect share capital and deposits from the members and borrow funds from SCARDBs. These banks are scrutinizing application received from the members lend the money for agricultural purposes and for non farming sectors. The performance of these PCARDBs at national level is analysed below.

Table 2.2

Performance of PCARDBs at National Level

(Rs. in Crore)

	2000-2001	*2001-2002*	*2002-2003*	*2003-2004*	*2004-2005*
Number	732	768 (4.91)	768 (0.00)	766 (-0.26)	768 (0.26)
Branches	718	1091 (51.94)	1008 (-7.60)	918 (-8.92)	932 (-1.52)
Owned funds	867	2494 (187.65)	2730 (9.46)	2141 (-21.57)	1782 (-16.76)
Deposits	234	256 (9.90)	222 (-13.28)	257 (15.76)	256 (-0.38)
Borrowings	8396	10334 (23.08)	11217 (8.54)	11917 (6.24)	12933 (8.52)
Loan Issued	1866	2045 (9.59)	2151 (5.18)	2164 (0.60)	2569 (18.71)
Loan outstanding	8380	9982 (19.11)	10775 (7.94)	11229 (4.21)	12719 (13.26)

Source : Compiled from Annual Reports of NABARD for various years.

Note: Figures in Parenthesis shows the percentage of change.

The total number of PCARDBS functioning in the country as on 2000–01 was 732. This has increased to 768 in 2004–05. The total owned funds of the PCARDBs also increased from Rs. 867 crores to 1782 crores during the study period. On the other hand there was marked increase in borrowings during the study period. i.e., from Rs. 8396 crores to 12933 crores. Consequent to this the total loan issued also increased from Rs. 1866 crores to Rs. 2569 crores during the study period.

Position of Non-performing Asset of SCARDBs and PCARDBs at National Level

The loan outstanding in Cooperative organizations at all levels is becoming a greater problem. Various reasons are attached for such out standings. Failure of crops, failure of monsoon, non integrity of members, lack of proper leadership and political problems are some of the reasons. The mounting of outstanding loans are shown on the Assets side of the Balance Sheet as an Asset. This is fictitious Assets bearing no value and for all practical purposes should be treat as a Non Performing Assets (NPA). The position of NPA in SCARDBs and PCARDBs at all India level is discussed below.

Table 2.3
NPA Position at All India Level

(Rs. in Crore)

Year	*Total NPA*		*Total Provision made*	
	SCARDB	*PCARDB*	*SCARDB*	*PCARDB*
2000-01	2850.56	2004.77	401.53	651.23
2001-02	2412.36 (-15.37)	3045.85 (51.93)	485.15 (20.82)	705.50 (8.39)
2002-03	3132.80 (29.86)	3008.81 (-10.21)	497.20 (2.48)	621.62 (-11.88)
2003-04	4318.55 (37.84)	3861.02 (28.32)	832.63 (62.46)	919.78 (47.96)
2004-05	5437.38 (25.90)	4055.91 (5.04)	1097.64 (31.82)	909.64 (-1.10)

Source: Compiled from Annual Reports of NABARD for various years.

Note: Figures in Parenthesis shows the percentage of change.

The loan outstanding was on the increasing trend indicating the poor recovery of loans. This is evident from the fact that the position of NPA both at SCARDB and PCARDB level have been on the increasing trend. The total NPA at SCARDBs level was Rs. 2850.56 crores in 2000–01, which has increased to Rs. 5437.38 crores in 2004–05. The respective figure for PCARDBs was Rs. 2004.77 crores and Rs. 4055.91 crores. These trends have worsened the financial visibility of ARDBs, because huge reserves in the form of provisioning are made due to NPAs.

Financial Structure of SCARDBs and PCARDBs in Tamilnadu

Finance is the blood of any financial institution. A commercial bank mobilizes funds through share capital and collection of deposits, but a cooperative bank has got one more source of funds which is called borrowing from Apex Banks. Hence the financial structure of cooperative banks consist of share capital, reserves, owned funds, deposits and borrowings as the source of funds for purposes of lending. These items will appear on the liabilities side of the Balance Sheet and on the assets side, items like investments, loans outstanding, NPA and other assets like furniture will appear. The financial structure of Tamilnadu SCARDBs and PCARDBs is analyzed in the following Table 2.4 and 2.5.

Table 2.4
Financial Structure of Tamilnadu SCARD Bank

(Rs. in Crore)

Particulars	*2001-02*	*2002-03*	*2003-04*	*2004-05*	*2005-06*
Share Capital	40.48	41.62 (2.81)	42.15 (1.27)	41.96 (-0.45)	40.38 (-3.76)
Reserves	36.38	37.59 (3.32)	38.87 (3.40)	40.17 (3.34)	41.61 (3.58)
Owned Funds	309.29	381.33 (23.29)	445.06 (16.71)	544.80 (22.41)	552.79 (1.46)
Deposits	37.85	44.09 (16.48)	53.32 (20.93)	54.33 (1.89)	48.52 (-10.69)
Investments	129.16	142.67 (10.45)	147.48	88.01 (3.37)	73.43 (-16.56)
Borrowings	1112.95	1197.64 (7.60)	1188.31 (0.77)	1030.24 (-13.30)	850.03 (-17.49)
Loan Outstanding	1183.31	1265.84 (6.97)	1260.22 (-0.44)	1139.58 (-9.57)	1008.42 (-11.50)
NPA	505.85	556.26 (9.96)	717.57 (28.59)	923.16 (-28.65)	892.75 (-3.29)
% of NPA	42.50	43.80 (3.05)	56.80 (29.68)	80.80 (42.25)	88.26 (9.23)
Provision for NPA	13.95	9.51 (-31.82)	26.81 (181.91)	35.63 (32.89)	11.22 (-68.50)
Cumulative Loss	-45.25	-45.67	-77.81	-131.24	-155.69

Source: Compiled from Annual Reports of TNSCARDBs, for various years.

Note: Figures in Parenthesis shows the percentage of change.

Table 2.5

Financial Structure of PCARDBs in Tamilnadu

(Rs. in lakhs)

Particulars	*2001-02*	*2002-03*	*2003-04*	*2004-05*	*2005-06*
Members	2112297	2113440	2135294	2125403	2012738
		(0.05)	(1.03)	(-0.46)	(-5.30)
Share Capital	9114.90	9442.24	9346.67	8178.87	7536.00
		(3.59)	(-1.01)	(-12.49)	(-7.86)
Reserves	30508.74	8683.77	8269.45	54175.78	7789.00
		(-71.53)	(-4.77)	(-34.48)	(43.77)
Working capital	138128.00	149659.00	152315.00	137379.00	113472.00
		(8.34)	(1.77)	(-9.80)	(-17.40)
Borrowings	119318.15	125633.50	125964.90	113957.82	99866.00
		(5.29)	(0.26)	(-9.53)	(-12.36)
Loan Outstanding	115311.73	122025.44	120052.42	104007.27	96402.03
		(-89.41)	(-1.61)	(-13.36)	(-7.31)
NPA	54533.24	60681.35	61859.81	66344.26	71821.81
		(11.27)	(1.94)	(7.25)	(8.25)
% of NPA	47.29	49.72	51.52	63.78	74.00
		(5.13)	(3.62)	(23.79)	(16.02)
Provision of NPA	11702.71	13489.04	13784.02	18026.04	19354.83
		(15.26)	(2.18)	(30.77)	(7.37)

Source: Compiled from Annual Reports of TNSCARDBs, for various years.

Note: Figures in Parenthesis shows the percentage of change.

In the case of Tamilnadu the LT structure consist of Tamilandu State Cooperative Agriculture and Rural Development Bank (TNSCARDB) and 181 PCARDBs. The financial indicator on the functioning of TNSCARDB shows that the increasing trend in NPA has severely hit the growth of the bank. The total NPA as on 2001–02 was Rs. 505.85

crores, Which has grown over the years and stood at Rs. 892.75 crores as on 2005–06, i.e., 88.26 percent to total loan was outstanding.

The cumulative loss of TNSCARDBs was also on the increasing trend for the study period, which was 45.25 crores in the year 2001–02 and gone to the extent of Rs. 155.69 crores in the year 2005–06.

There are 181 PCARDBs functioning in Tamilnadu. The area of operation of a PCARDB generally covers two or three revenue blocks or one taluk. As on 2001–02 total number of members admitted by these banks was 2112297. All these banks have not made any significant performance during the study period. The growth of NPAs has been a major concern, which erodes the financial soundness of the banks and blocks the flow of funds.

Loans issued by Primary Cooperative Agriculture and Rural Development Banks at Tamilnadu Level

The main function of a bank is receiving deposits and lending money. A cooperative bank at ground level borrows funds from Apex Bank and lends the same to members for productive purposes. The extent of loan issued by PCARDBs at Tamilnadu level is analyzed for the study period in the following Table.

Table 2.6

Loan Issued in Tamilnadu at PCARDB Level

(Rs. in Lakhs)

Year	*Total Loan*	*Growth Rate*
2000-01	20093.43	--
2001-02	19240.51	- 4.24
2002-03	21791.62	13.25
2003-04	12700.25	- 4171
2004-05	1243.96	-90.20

Source: Compiled from Annual Reports of NABARD for various years.

Note: Figures in Parenthesis shows the percentage of change.

The ground level credit flow at PCARDBs level in Tamilnadu is given in Table 2.6. A general recession in the loan operations of PCARDBS was found during the study period. This was due to Government waiving policies and consequent impact on recovery and recycling of funds. For example the total loan issued during the year 2000–01 was Rs. 20093.43 lakhs, which was 0.60 per cent less than the previous year. The total loan issued during the year 2004 – 05 was Rs. 1243.96 lakhs, which was 90.20 percent less than the previous year. From the above analysis, it is found that the functions of ARDBs structure at all levels have been severely affected. The reasons for this morbid growth are:

1. Loan waiving policies of the Governments.
2. Entry of new generation banks in rural finance, and
3. Politicization and bureaucratizes of cooperative movement.

Functioning of PCARDBs in Sample Districts

The trends in the functioning of ARDBs have its influence at micro level also. The PCARDBs in sample districts were registered during colonial period itself. The functions of these PCARDBs are analyzed hereunder.

Membership

As per the provisions of the Tamilnadu Cooperative Societies Act 1983 and Rules 1988, all the persons who are competent to contract, residing in the area of operation of the PCARDBs and willing to avail the services are eligible to become the members. Land owners as well as tenants are admitted as members of the PCARDBs. Lift irrigation societies can also become members of PCARDBs. Though for providing loan to NFS landed property is not required, the banks insist the landed property for the purpose of security. However, during the study it was found that in both the sample districts, after the introduction of NFS loans, the numbers of members in sample PCARDBs increased. On the other hand there are certain specific problems with regard to membership in ARDBs. According the Task Force 2006 the problems are:

- Membership is limited and not stable owing to the limited investment credit needs of farmers
- Large area of operation entails higher transaction cost for the structure as well as the members
- Existing borrowers are unable to meet their different credit needs from a single point.
- These problems have bred three types of members (individuals) in the PCARDBs. They are viz.,
  - Those who are dormant, either because they never took a loan or they cleared the loan and continue to retain membership without any further loans
  - Those who are continuing to be borrowers, but have limited contact with the banks because the transactions are reduced to repaying an occasional installment, and
  - Those who are recent borrowers.

The position of membership in Sample PCARDBs is discussed below.

While analyzing the performance PCARDBs with regard to coverage of membership it was found that Mayiladuthurai PCARDB faired better while comparing their counterparts in Nagapattinam district. In the case of Dindugal district, Dindugal PCARDB faired better than others. As the growth of membership is directly linked with the loan operations the growth in membership picturing the growth of the bank.

Share Capital

Every member while joining in the bank should subscribe share capital of the bank. The value of each share is Rs.100 and the entrance fee is Rs.10. Share capital forms the owned fund of the bank and decides the borrowing power of the bank. Apart from this share contribution, every member is required to subscribe the share capital of the bank at the time of availing of loans. Usually this share capital

Table 2.7

Position of Membership in sample PCARDBs

(Figures in Numbers)

Year	Nagapattinam				Dindugal						
	Mayila-duthurai	*Sirkali*	*Vedharanyam*	*Avg.*	*Dindugal*	*Kodai-kanal*	*Oddan-chatram*	*Palani*	*Rediyar-chathiram*	*Vedacha-ndur*	*Avg.*
2001-02	13582	8167	9608	10452	7912	3639	5820	7107	5813	8651	6490
2002-03	13873	8306	9901	10693	7852	3848	8621	6779	6843	5117	6510
2003-04	13914	8354	9928	10732	7960	3943	9529	6994	7094	5898	6903
2004-05	13908	8354	9940	10734	7783	4047	9684	7015	7146	5997	6945
2005-06	13145	8350	9940	10478	7782	4039	9599	7015	7140	5990	6927

Source : Compiled from Annual Reports and Audit Reports of the sample banks.

Table 2.8

Position of Share Capital in Sample PCARDBs

(Rupees in Lakhs)

Year	Nagapattinam				Dindugal						
	Mayila-duthurai	*Sirkali*	*Vedharanyam*	*Avg.*	*Dindugal*	*Kodai-kanal*	*Oddan-chatram*	*Palani*	*Rediyar-chathiram*	*Vedacha-ndur*	*Avg.*
2001-02	65.24	34.69	51.16	50.36	45.00	29.41	34.05	55.50	34.98	58.00	42.82
2002-03	70.25	37.03	56.00	54.42	42.32	33.78	50.62	53.93	56.78	68.93	51.06
2003-04	63.74	35.06	53.78	50.86	39.61	40.68	64.39	70.00	64.32	39.61	53.10
2004-05	57.56	32.49	49.87	46.64	41.43	39.56	67.67	72.17	65.41	41.76	54.66
2005-06	50.63	30.97	45.39	42.33	40.47	27.48	60.41	68.41	63.39	39.92	50.01

Source: Compiled from Annual Reports and Audit Reports of the sample banks.

Diagram 2.1

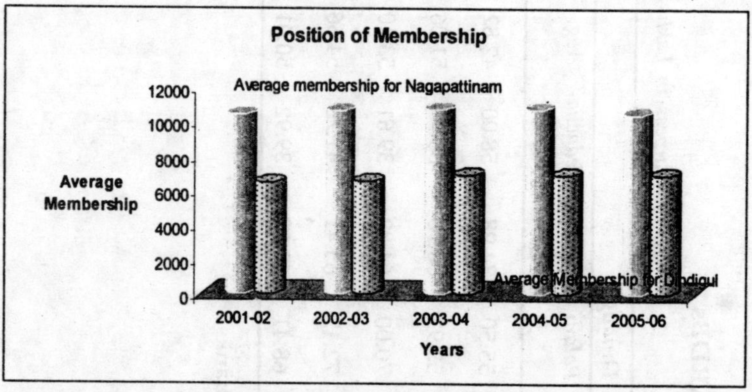

Diagram 2.2

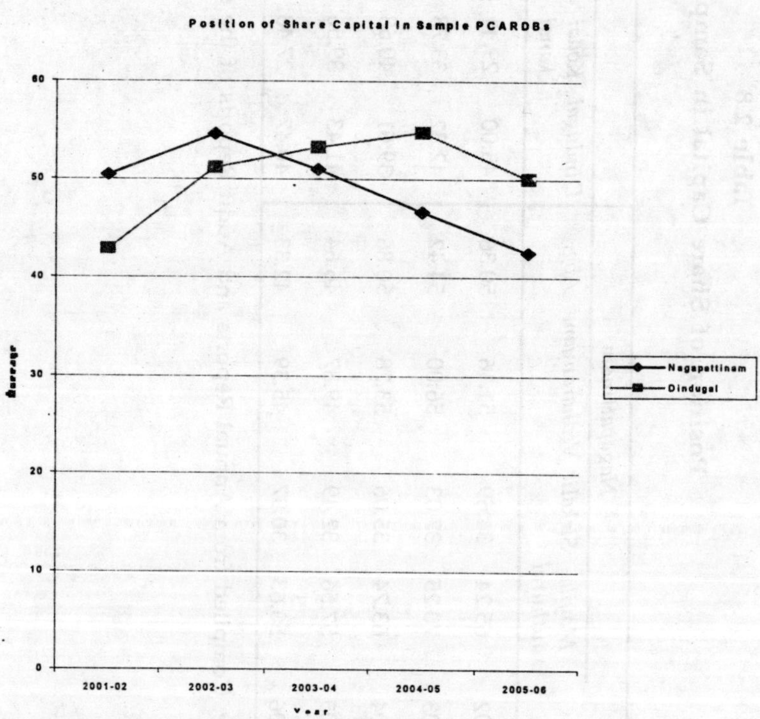

Table 2.9

Position of Reserve Fund in sample PCARDBs

(Rupees in Lakhs)

Year	*Nagapattinam*				*Dindugal*						
	Mayila-duthurai	*Sirkali*	*Vedharanyam*	*Avg.*	*Dindugal*	*Kodai-kanal*	*Oddan-chatram*	*Palani*	*Rediyar-chathiram*	*Vedacha-ndur*	*Avg.*
2001-02	1.78	17.93	0.88	6.86	128.69	7.86	60.01	2.70	2.69	2.70	34.11
2002-03	1.29	17.98	0.88	6.72	121.63	9.11	59.61	1.51	3.67	1.83	32.89
2003-04	1.29	18.06	0.88	6.74	123.63	11.63	3.67	1,52	5.19	2.63	24.71
2004-05	0.76	18.06	0.88	6.57	123.63	9.81	10.87	1.52	5.17	2.51	25.58
2005-06	1.96	18.06	0.88	6.96	123.63	9.82	10.87	1.31	5.17	2.51	25.55

Source: Compiled from Annual Reports and Audit Reports of the sample banks.

contribution ranges from 5 per cent to 10 per cent of the loan to be availed. As opined by the Task Force 2006 as the long term loan needs of farmers are rather infrequent, there is neither any incentive nor occasion for the members to voluntarily contribute any further capital to the structure. In the ST credit structure, however, where the client member has regular transactions, the share capital could increase every time a fresh and higher loan is sought. In addition, the structure at both the primary and apex levels has share capital contribution from the State Government. Generally State Government's contribution to share capital exceeds the share capital contributed by the members in the bank.

The trend in the position of paid up share capital of PCARDB in Nagapattinam district shows that Mayiladuthurai PCARDB faired better than their counterparts by mobilizing paid up share capital to the tune of Rs. 50.63 lakhs as on 2005–06. However it is in the declining trend from 2002–03 onwards.

The trend in the position of paid up share capital of the PCARDBs in Dindugal shows that Palani PCARDBs could be able to mobilize share capital more than the district average, during the study period. Though Reddiyarchatram PCARDB maintained high proportion of borrowing members compared to others they could not mobilize shares like others throughout the study period.

Reserve Fund

It is mandatory for every cooperative society to create statutory reserve fund and other reserves out of the profit earned every year. The very objective of this fund is to meet any unforeseen losses to the society in future. Further, certain portions of reserve fund (not invested amount) are used as owned fund, which form part of working capital.

While analyzing the performance of PCARDBs in the creation of reserve fund, it was found that Sirkali PCARDB created more reserve fund than others in Nagapattinam district. Whereas in Dindugal district compared to the reserve position in other PCARDB, the reserve position in Dindugal PCARDB was better.

Diagram 2.3

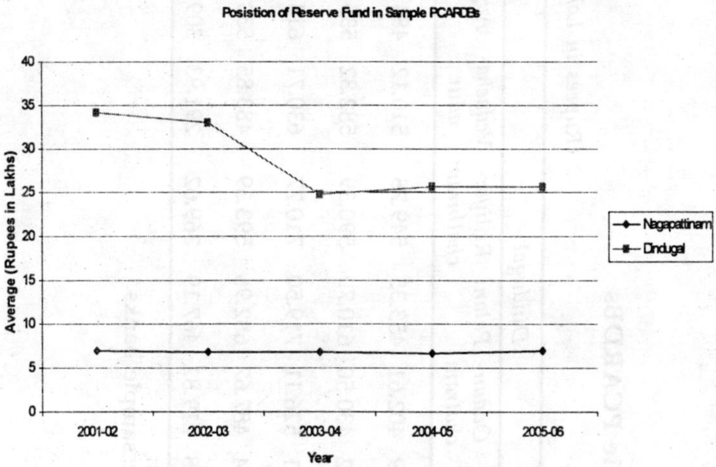

Borrowed Funds

Borrowings constitute the major portion of the working capital of the PCARDBs. The SCARDB and DCCB are the main sources of borrowings. As majority of the PCARDBs in the State do not accept any kind of deposits either from the members or from the public, PCARDBs should depend on the higher financial institutions for borrowings. The study Group on Deposit Mobilization by ARDBs (Bhandari Committee, 1996) suggested that the ARDBs should be allowed procuring term deposits of wider range. Even then many ARDBs are reluctant to this suggestion and still depend upon the higher tiers for refinance. This increases the cost of capital for the ARDBs.

It was found that the average borrowing per bank at district level was Rs.309.03 lakhs in Dindugal district in 2005-06. Palani PCARDBs was found to have borrowed more than district average during the study period. Also, it was found that there is high correlation between borrowings and loan issued at the district level. It shows that the PCARDBs depend upon only borrowing from SCARDB as a major source for lending.

Table 2.10

Position of Borrowings in sample PCARDBs

(Rupees in Lakhs)

Year	*Nagapattinam*				*Dindugal*						
	Mayila-duthurai	*Si-kali*	*Vedharanyam*	*Avg.*	*Dindugal*	*Kodai-kanal*	*Oddan-chatram*	*Palani*	*Rediyar-chathiram*	*Vedacha-ndur*	*Avg.*
2001-02	1345.51	547.35	768.01	886.95	592.24	399.69	402.61	453.35	549.78	510.12	484.63
2002-03	1178.81	534.68	821.64	845.04	589.23	410.82	430.50	610.70	590.39	582.32	535.66
2003-04	1042.89	463.31	863.65	789.95	589.62	501.61	526.11	719.50	710.77	630.71	613.05
2004-05	928.80	413.88	796.26	712.98	501.17	450.74	487.67	682.96	593.39	483.85	533.29
2005-06	798.86	394.76	786.40	660.00	209.24	296.38	219.82	467.19	369.62	291.93	309.03

Source: Compiled from Annual Reports and Audit Reports of the sample banks.

Diagram 2.4

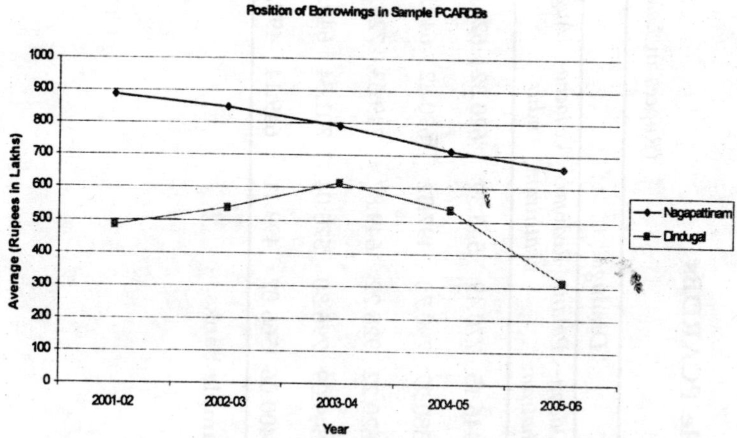

The position of borrowings in PCARDBs in Ngapattinam district shows decreasing trend over the years. The condition was worse in the case of Sirkali PCARDB. This trend will have negative effect on the loan portfolio.

Working Capital

The owned fund (other than invested portion) and borrowed fund constitute the working capital for the PCARDBs. It was found that as PCARDBs are not concentrating on deposits in the sample districts, borrowing constitutes major portion to working capital. Though the SCARDB favored for the deposit mobilization at PCARDB level, it seems that no initiative have been taken so far in this regard. Even at the SCARDBs level dependency on external sources of finance is high. SCARDBs float debentures with State Government guarantee. These debentures are subscribed to the extent of 90 per cent to 95 per cent by NABARD and the balance is shared by the State Government and the Government of India. Unlike the higher tiers of ST structure SCARDBs did not raise member or non-member deposits on any significant scale. In these respects there is not much difference between the federal, unitary and mixed models of LT structure.

Table 2.11

Position of Working Capital in sample PCARDBs

(Rupees in Lakhs)

Year	Nagapattinam				Dindugal						
	Mayila-duthurai	*Sirkali*	*Vedharanyam*	*Avg.*	*Dindugal*	*Kodai-kanal*	*Oddan-chatram*	*Palani*	*Rediyar-chathiram*	*Vedacha-ndur*	*Avg.*
2001-02	1253.15	772.29	833.95	953.13	767.62	596.49	446.15	770.49	543.39	620.32	624.07
2002-03	1310.49	764.89	896.05	990.47	771.32	511.09	580.27	790.70	497.32	690.82	640.25
2003-04	1108.15	694.82	940.24	914.40	876.92	549.47	620.22	928.22	649.87	749.63	729.05
2004-05	987.35	645.54	866.03	832.97	799.85	476.12	549.09	796.30	576.04	701.84	649.87
2005-06	857.67	592.39	786.48	745.51	515.94	356.19	400.06	566.07	499.11	649.14	497.75

Source: Compiled from Annual Reports and Audit Reports of the sample banks.

Diagram 2.5

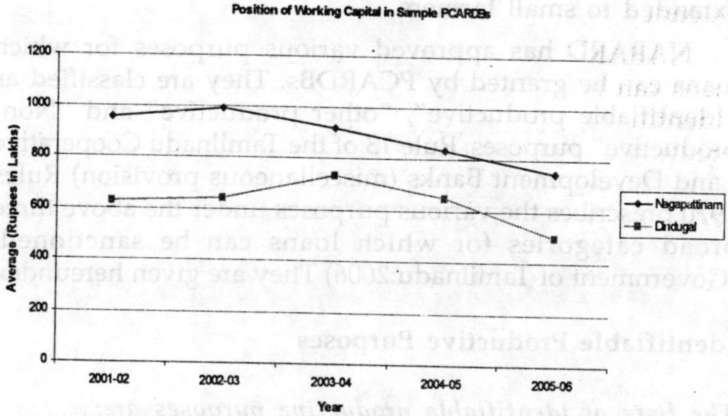

The trend in the working capital in PCARDBs in Dindugal district shows that the Vedasandur PCARDB followed by Palani PCARDB has higher level of working capital than the district average i.e., Rs. 497.75 lakhs.

The trends in the working capital position of PCARDBs in Nagapattinam district shows that the position of working capital in Mayiladuthurai PCARDB is better than its counterparts in the district.

Management

As a Government policy the elected board of management of PCARDBs was superseded and Government officials are appointed as Special Officers to manage the affairs of the sample banks. The special officers are assisted by a team of paid employees of concerned PACRDBs. At present only three cadre of paid employees are in service viz., Secretary, Supervisors and Office Assistants. This structure has also been rationalized and at present the service of Office Assistants is out sourced.

Total Loan Disbursed by the PCARDBs

Sample banks provide loans on the security of the unencumbered landed property. Loans were issued to the landowners in almost all villages in the area of operation. As a matter of policy 60 percent of financial assistance was extended to small farmers.

NABARD has approved various purposes for which loans can be granted by PCARDBs. They are classified as "Identifiable productive", "other productive" and "Non-productive" purposes. Rule 13 of the Tamilnadu Cooperative Land Development Banks (miscellaneous provision) Rules 1970 prescribes the various purposes under the above three broad categories for which loans can be sanctioned. (Government of Tamilnadu:2006) They are given hereunder.

Identifiable Productive Purposes

The lists of identifiable productive purposes are;

(i) Sinking of new wells (surface wells, dug-cum-bore wells, tube wells and filter points)

(ii) Construction of new tanks to conserve water for wet cultivation.

(iii) Deepening of existing wells, repairs of old wells (surface wells) and deepening reconstruction of or repairs to tanks.

(iv) Construction of field channels & pump house.

(v) Purchase and installation of pump sets (diesel or electrical), deposits with State Electricity Boards for high or low tension lines for energizing electric motors.

(vi) Purchase of tractors, trailors, power tillers, sprayers, paddy thrashers and other agricultural machinery and implements.

(vii) Construction of godowns, cattle shed, farmhouses, manure sheds, tobacco barns etc.

(viii) Barbed wire fencing.

(ix) Drying-cum thrashing floors.

Other Productive Purposes

The other productive purposes included in the list are:

(i) Leveling, bunding and reclamation of lands.

(ii) Soil conservation by terracing.

(iii) Construction of drainage channel to prevent flooding or bunding of land to prevent erosion.

(iv) Preparation of land for orchards, plantation etc.

Non–Productive Purpose

There are certain purposes, which are not directly productive but capacitate the borrowers. They are:

(i) Loans for redemption of prior debts, mortgages,

(ii) Purchase of tenancy, ownership rights and,

(iii) Purchase of land.

Loans are advanced on the mortgage of agricultural lands, the lands to be benefited by the proposed development have to be invariable offered as security. In the case of loans for the purchase of a tractor the tractor is taken as a collateral security by insisting on the "C" certificated being in the joint names of the borrower and the PCARDB.

Valuation

From November 1971 onwards, a uniform method of valuation at 8 times the post development income is being adopted in respect of loans for purpose which generate additional income. However in the case of loans for purchase of tractor and power tillers, the market value of land as per the guideline figures of the Registration Department is adopted. In respect of loans for construction of godowns, cattle shed, farm houses, thrashing yards, manure shed and animal husbandry etc., where no additional income is generated, the valuation is arrived at 50 percent of the guideline value.

The TNSCARDB has prescribed the district wise norms in respect of cost of cultivation yield, gross income and net income of principal crops. The valuation officers should value the land adopting the norms prescribed by the TNSCSADB.

Loan Eligibility and Repaying Capacity

Loan eligibility is assessed at 50 percent of the value of land. In case of tractor and power tillers the cost of machinery is added to the cost of land for working out the eligibility but the loan amount is not to exceed the value of the land.

Down Payment

In order that the borrower has a stake in the project, he is required to contribute a portion of the cost of the project as down payment at a certain percentage of project cost. The down payment may be in the form of cash or labour contributed by the borrower and his family members. The down payments exclude share capital contribution

Disbursement of Loan Installment

The PCARDBs are permitted to sanction loans upto Rs. 2 Lakhs at PCARDBs level for normal loans. The NFS loan application amount exceeding Rs. 2 Lakhs should be sent to the branch of the TNSCARDB for sanction. Loan for development purpose are normally disbursed in three installments (30 percent, 40 percent and 30 percent of the loan amount). Subsequent installments are disbursed only after the full and proper utilization of the earlier installments. In case of loans for purchase of tractors and power tillers, electric motors and pump sets, diesel engines and pump sets and any other agricultural machinery, the disbursement is effected in one lump-sum to the dealer direct against the invoice and delivery note. The disbursement in case of loans for electric motor pump sets and diesel engine pump sets is made to the dealer only after the installation of the pump set / diesel engines. The same is verified by the Land Valuation and Estimation Officer attached to the PCARDBs. Loans are advanced for electric motor, pump sets which are on the approved list of the TNSCARDB.

Loans are advanced only to those diesel engines which bear I.S.I. markings. In respect of NFS loans machineries should be verified by the Junior Engineer/Assistant Engineer of TNSCARDB.

Utilization

The TNSCARDB has prescribed the following time limit for the utilization of loans for different purposes.

Sl. No.	*Purpose*	*Time Limit for Utilization*
1.	(a) Wells with pumpsets	3 months for utilization of each installment from the date of disbursement.
2.	(b) Reclamation of land	3 months for utilization of each installment from the date of disbursement.
3.	(c) Plantations	One year from the date on which the first installment for that year was disbursed.

Explicit recital should be made in the mortgage bond as clause 3(A) to the effect that failure to adhere to the time limit will entail foreclosure of the loans.

Fees Payable by Borrowers

Every borrower should pay certain amount of fees for availing loans. They are:

Evaluation Fees

An evaluation fee at 1 percent of the cost of the project is collected for all loans. Fees for legal opinion and technical estimate are met from out of this. However, applicant has to remit legal fees at Rs. 2/ per every Rs. 1,000/- of loan amount subject to a minimum of Rs. 5/- and maximum of Rs. 40/-. This item is treated as miscellaneous income and not suspense repayable at bank level.

Encumbrance Certificate Fees

Encumbrance Certificate fees for 13 years is Rs. 44/-. No fee is payable for loan applications upto Rs. 50000/-. Members of schedule castes and scheduled tribes are totally exempted from the payment of encumbrance fees.

Registration Fees

A registration fee is collected at 1 percent of the loan amount. Members of scheduled caste and scheduled tribes are exempted from the payment of the registration fees.

Diagram 2.6

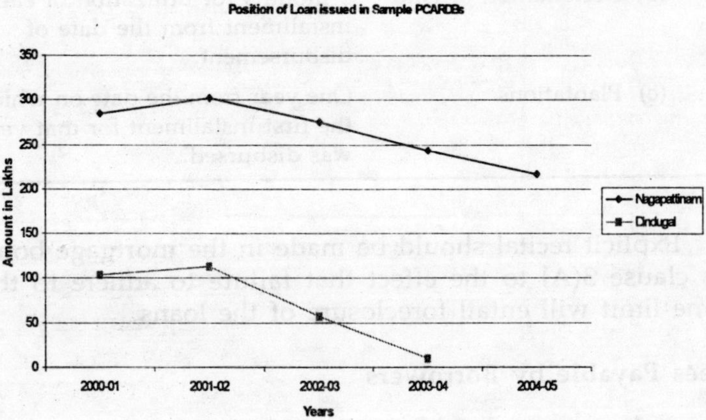

The performance in loan operation of sample PCARDBs shows morbid growth. It was found that the total loan issued by the Sirkali PCARDB in Nagapattinam and Palani PCARDBs in Dindugal district have provided loan more than their respective counterparts. Further, it is to be noted here that from the year 2004 – 05 Kodaikanal PCARDB from 2005–06 all PCARDBs in Dindugal district have not provided any loans due to poor recovery climate.

Table 2.12

Position of Loan Issued in Sample PCARDBs

(Rupees in Lakhs)

Year	*Nagapattinam*				*Dindugal*						
	Mayiladuthurai	*Sirkali*	*Vedharanyam*	*Avg.*	*Dindugal*	*Kodaikanal*	*Oddanchatram*	*Palani*	*Rediyarchathiram*	*Vedachandur*	*Avg.*
2001-02	223.39	473.59	157.59	284.85	80.34	53.23	90.99	150.94	93.13	153.03	103.61
2002-03	180.54	521.49	202.01	301.35	126.22	54.40	96.91	126.33	101.05	173.32	113.03
2003-04	39.72	548.14	235.49	274.45	80.44	32.45	28.22	73.38	63.55	59.78	56.30
2004-05	10.60	509.15	207.58	242.44	3.31	NIL	6.51	17.21	10.88	14.59	8.75
2005-06	1.60	459.00	186.18	215.59	NIL	NIL	NIL	NIL	NIL	NIL	--

Source: Compiled from Annual Reports and Audit Reports of the sample banks.

Recovery of Loans

The due dates for annual repayment of loans by the borrowers are: 1st February, 1st May and 1st November. PCARDBs are empowered to restrain and sell the produce of the mortgaged loan including standing crops for recovery of annual installments. The banks have further been empowered to avail the summary procedures for recovery of loan as arrears of land revenue under Revenue Recovery Act. However, due to waiving policies of the State Government the recovery climate is volatile to banking system which resulted in increasing trend in overdue.

It was found that the position of overdue in sample PCARDBs in Nagapattinam district was more than eighty percent to demand in the year 2006. Individual bank wise analysis shows that though the total overdue has comedown over the years in the case of Mayiladuthurai PCARDB, its position in demand has been at higher level. The condition was severe in the case of Vadharanyam PCARDB.

Diagram 2.7

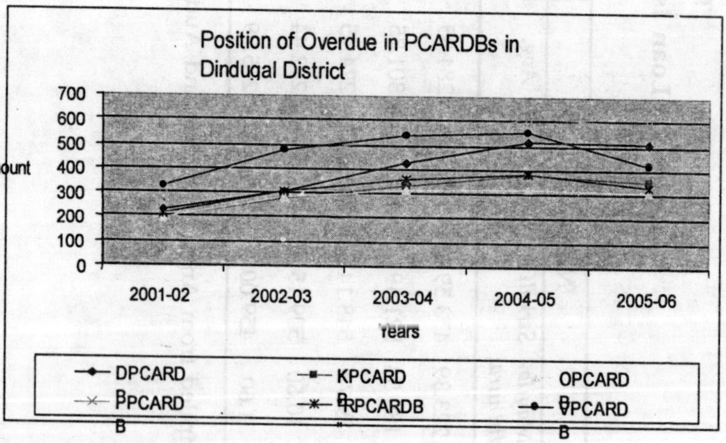

Table 2.13
Position of Overdue in Sample PCARDBs

(Rupees in Lakhs)

S. No.	Name of the PCARD Bank	2001 – 2002 Demand	2001 – 2002 Overdue	2002 – 2003 Demand	2002 – 2003 Overdue	2003 – 2004 Demand	2003 – 2004 Overdue	2004 – 2005 Demand	2004 – 2005 Overdue	2005 – 2006 Demand	2005 – 2006 Overdue
1.	Mayiladuthurai	749.33	607.33 (81.04)	623.26	444.64 (71.34)	636.59	446.47 (70.13)	601.02	452.54 (75.29)	560.31	463.41 (82.70)
2.	Sirkali	283.13	197.41 (69.72)	304.75	229.82 (75.41)	320.66	246.80 (76.96)	397.51	247.48 (62.25)	360.00	314.59 (87.38)
3.	Vedharanyam	408.66	331.39 (81.09)	486.05	394.81 (81.22)	553.74	452.37 (81.69)	578.24	498.94 (86.28)	589.58	557.73 (94.59)
4.	Dindugal	289.40	226.37 (78.22)	414.53	306.01 (73.82)	585.60	423.51 (72.32)	601.03	513.37 (85.41)	588.63	506.11 (85.98)
5.	Kodaikanai	267.88	196.12 (73.21)	398.95	279.35 (70.02)	489.87	333.75 (68.13)	543.32	379.19 (69.79)	447.40	351.12 (78.48)
6.	Oddanchatram	245.18	196.25 (80.04)	374.81	287.22 (76.63)	424.60	315.44 (74.29)	400.31	321.81 (80.39)	350.90	313.04 (89.21)
7	Palani	366.16	316.11 (86.33)	575.04	467.05 (81.22)	672.52	525.38 (78.12)	611.02	590.11 (96.57)	647.89	591.01 (91.22)
8	Rediyarchathiram	268.48	213.12 (79.33)	415.84	306.35 (73.67)	510.92	356.98 (69.87)	572.96	382.68 (66.79)	449.61	334.11 (74.31)
9	Vedachandur	366.91	325.16 (88.62)	574.12	478.19 (83.29)	688.25	537.94 (78.16)	689.92	552.56 (80.09)	476.97	419.12 (87.87)

Source : Compiled from Annual Reports and Audit Reports of the sample banks.

Diagram 2.8

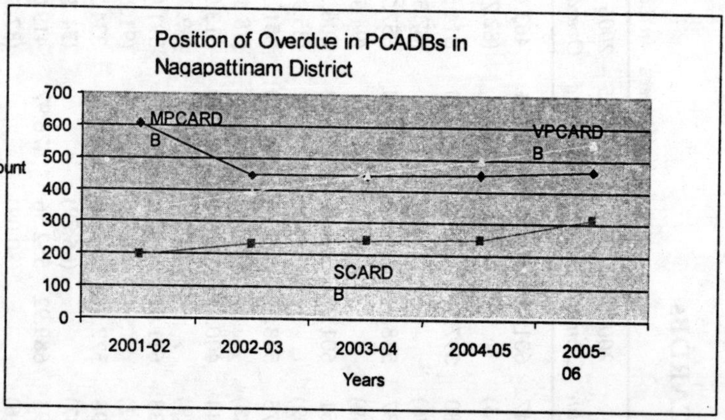

Challenges Ahead

The above analysis shows that the performance in the business of ARDBs shows complex trend. It means neither the apex institution nor the primaries are viable. In the case of PCARDBs in Dindugal district during the 2005-06, there was virtually no new lending. When the primary function is paralyzed, how could the system operate?. This is only the ice berg. There are many more PCARDBs functioning in the country. This scenario attracts new challenges before ARDBs.

Increasing Cost of capital

As PCARDBs depend upon their apex tier for resources, the cost of working capital has been on a rising trend. If local low cost resources are mobilized the cost of working capital can be reduced. Keeping in view the trend at national level the Task Force 2006 has suggested the following measures for reducing the cost of capital.

- Allow the PCARDBs to access all types of deposits from members.
- Allow PCARDBs to borrow from any regulated financial institutions including federal units of the ST structure.

- Allow SCARDBs to mobilize public deposits under suitable regulatory and supervisory arrangements.

If all these suggestions are implemented in Tamilnadu, it would benefit the entire sample PCARDBs to strengthen their capital structure.

Role of Government

After the introduction of new economic policy, the Government role in promoting and supporting the cooperatives has been reduced. However, the duel control mechanism still exits. Cooperatives in general and PCARDBs in particular have been continuously affected by politicization and bureaucratization. For example in India:

- No elections have been held in both SCARDBs/ PCARDBs for 10 years or more in three states.
- Boards of 10 out of 20 SCARDBs and 414 out of 768 PCARDBs have been superseded (2003-04).
- Most State Governments combine the roles of dominant shareholder, manager, regulator and concurrent supervisor and auditor.
- The Department headed by the Registrar of Cooperative Societies (RCS) can and does influence administrative matters. The interference is in the form of supersession of boards, appointment of administrators or special officers (Tamilnadu) and assuming powers to approve staffing patterns, recruitment, emoluments, asset purchase pattern, etc.
- Some of the State Governments also interfere in matters relating to fixing rates of interest on loans, either directly or indirectly.
- The State Governments also announce waivers of principal and interest quite often and such waiver amounts even when released, are passed on with a time lag.
- The impairment of the governance structure is also because of politicization and lack of professionalism in these institutions. The numbers of directors on

boards of SCARDBs, who have professional qualifications, are few.

Under these conditions if the ARDBs are not allowed to function freely in the competitive environment, their survival will be questioned in the very near future.

Entry of New Generation Banks in rural areas

The liberalization process breeds number of modern banking institutions which are providing door to door services in rural areas. Nowadays they pose heavy threat to the existing cooperative banking edifice in mobilizing and deployment of resources by utilizing modern management techniques. They use globally tested strategies to win in the market. This trend is the major threat before PCARDBs.

The Success of Self-Help Groups

Self-Help Groups (SHGs) have become a movement. Their successes have shown that the small borrowers quit their cooperatives and join hands with the SHGs to borrow and save money. All the rural financial institutions have harvested these opportunities and established a niche in the market. Already ST structure has successfully demonstrated bank linkages with the SHGs. ARDBs structure should also be permitted to act as Self Help group Promoting Institutions (SHPI) so as to promote SHGs as well as provide financial linkage. There are more than 10,000 SHGs functioning in sample districts and still there is greater scope list to form and provide financial linkage to SHGs.

Conclusion

The foregoing analysis shows that the socio, economic and infrastructural facilities available in the sample districts are bankable. It means there is greater scope for any financial institutions to expand its market. The role of cooperatives in general and PCARDBs in particular in the socio – economic development of the State need not be over emphasized. In fact the first PACS was registered in Thirur village of Tamilnadu soon after the enactment of Cooperative Credit

Societies Act in 1904. In this context, all the PCARDBs in sample district were registered during colonial era itself. With the long years of experience in rural finance, sample PCARDBs have contributed to the socio–economic development of the sample districts by providing the needed long term finance. This was found during interactions held with the sample respondents. However, the anti cooperative policies of the successive State Governments (not allowing cooperatives to function fully and freely as per ICA Principles), and its impact on the perceptions of general public on the functions of ARDBs have affected the functions of ARDBs. These trends have affected the business of sample PCARDBs. But, the emergence of NFS, as absorber of excessive workforce in rural areas, provides scope for expansion of business of PCARDBs. With this background the next chapter analyses the role of sample PCARDBs in the promotion of NFS.

3

Business Policies and Performance of PCARDBs with special Reference to Non Farm Sector Loans

The traditional image of farm households in developing countries has been that they focus almost exclusively on farming and undertake little rural non-farm (NF) activity. This image persists and is widespread even today. Policy debate still tends to equate farm income with rural incomes, and rural/urban relations with farm/non-farm relations (Usha Tuteja; 2004)

Nevertheless, there are mounting evidences that NF income (i.e. income derived in this sector from wage-paying activities and self-employment in commerce, manufacturing and other services) is an important resource for farm and other rural households, including the landless poor as well as rural town residents.

There are several reasons why the promotion of NF activity can be of great interest to policy-makers of developing country. First, the evidence shows that NF income is an important factor in household economies in food security, since it allows greater access to food. This source of income may also prevent rapid or excessive urbanization as well as natural resource degradation through overexploitation.

Second, in the face of credit constraints, NF activity affects the performance of agriculture by providing farmers with cash to invest in productivity-enhancing inputs. Furthermore, development of NF activity in the food system (including agro processing, distribution and the provision of farm inputs) may increase the profitability of farming by increasing the availability of inputs and improving access to market outlets. In turn, better performance of food system increases rural income and lowers urban food prices.

Third, the nature and performance of agriculture, themselves affected by agricultural policies, can have important effects on the dynamism of the NF sector to the extent that the latter is linked to agriculture. This sector grows fast and most equitably where agriculture is dynamic –where farm output is available for processing and distribution (Lanjouw and Lanjouw : 1995, Kishore C Samal 1997), where there are inputs to be sold and equipment repaired and where farm cash incomes are spent on local goods and services.

Realizing the importance of NFS, Government and Banking Sector gave adequate importance to promote NFS by formulating various schemes/programmes in the country. The District Rural Industries Project (DRIP) is one among them. DRIP is an integrated area based project for the development of NFS through credit intensification process in collaboration with project partners to provide sustainable employment opportunities to rural population by facilitating setting up of cottage, village, tiny and small industries in the rural areas.

The DRIP aims at removal of constraints/weakness in the development of NFS in an organized manner mainly through the use of existing promotional and financial instrument with the association and cooperation of the State Government, Voluntary Agencies, promotional, developmental and credit agencies in the field. NABARD launched the project in five districts selected from five regions on a pilot basis in 1993-94. Development of NFS through

DRIP was with the objectives of:

- Employment generation;
- Integration of agriculture and non agriculture;
- Harness of local skill / traditional craftsmanship;
- Exploitation of local minerals;
- Promotion of value addition and product diversification;
- Promote entrepreneurial culture;
- Promote women oriented NFS, village and cottage industries; and
- Empower village artisans, craftsmen etc. through appropriate interventions.

The project envisages drawing up of realistic action plan for the relevant sectors/areas in the district to be implemented over a period of five years with credit from the banking sector, integrated with relevant linkages needed and other non-financial services provided by various identified agencies. The action plan envisaged in project included:

- Strategic planning for rural non farm sector development – broad basing and integrating Farm Sector and Non Farm Sector
- Evolving responsive institutions for effective escort services and entrepreneur development
- Policy focus for preferred rural enterprise with large local employment potential
- Involvement of Non Governmental Organizations (NGOs) and corporate adoptions for technology transfer Market support and empowering artisans
- Involvement of producers' associations in the policy framing exercise as well as in the planning process
- Capacity building of rural financial institutions and entrepreneurs
- Specific infrastructural support such as training–cum–production centers

Active involvement of Government and non-governmental agencies were necessitated for the success of the project. Government Departments like Industries, Agriculture, Horticulture, Sericulture, agencies like District Industries Centre, District Rural Development Agency, Khadi and Village Industries Commission (KVIC), Small Industries Service Institute (SISI), Non Government Organizations, Voluntary Agencies, Product Boards, Producers Forums etc., were to actively participate in the project.

In addition to cent per cent refinance of loans issued under DRIP, NABARD, in association with partner agencies, organized a good number of promotional programmes in DRIP district for promotion and development of the NFS during the project period. The efforts under DRIP has resulted in setting up of a good number of new NFS units, enhanced employment opportunities, increased Ground Level Credit (GLC) flow and also improved refinance disbursement by NABARD under NFS in the district. Since the project has completed three years, considerable credit has been disbursed and sizable amount has been spent on account of promotional programmes, with these background the potential for NFS activities in the selected districts are analyzed hereunder so as to evaluate the performance of sample PCARDBs in distribution of NFS loans.

Potentialities of NFS activities in Dindugal District

In Tamilnadu, the contribution of agriculture (inclusive of crop, livestock, fisheries and forestry) to Net State Domestic Product (NSDP) has been declining over the last few decades. Whereas agriculture accounted for 53.37 percent of NSDP in 1950-2001, it accounts for only 16.65 per cent in 2001–02. On the other hand, the share of the secondary and tertiary sectors has increased from 13.72 per cent and 33 percent, respectively in 1950–01 to 31.04 per cent and 49.31 percent in 2001–02 (NABARD: 2007-08).

Development of Non Farm Sector is synonymous to Rural Development. The Non Farm Sector holds the key to unlocking the huge employment potential in rural areas. The NFS activities foster entrepreneurship in rural areas thereby acts as a deterrent to flux of migration from rural to urban areas. The achievements, success stories and the scale of employment generation in NFS in rural areas are not only a matter of statistics but verifiable and quantifiable indicators.

As a drought prone district there is scope for the development of NFS activities in Dindugal district. Because there were a total of 973332 workers in the district as per census 2001 out of which 274056 were urban workers and 320300 other workers. There were 25180 workers in household industry and 131439 were marginal unskilled workers. They mainly depended on NFS activities. Thus the district has adequate work force to support the activity. The number of workers in the organized industrial sector was 37902. Employment in working factories during 2004-05 was 29246.

Hence the growth and health of the NFS is vital to ensure absorption of additional work force dependent on agriculture. There were 87 medium and large scale industries in the district as on 2004-05. There were 5 industrial societies in the district viz., Lock Workers' Industrial Society, Polythene Workers' Industrial Society, Small Service Industrial Society, Auto Workers' Industrial Society, Kurumbapatti Metal Workers' Industrial Society. Two of these industrial societies are dormant. Of the three working industrial societies, two are working in profit.

The Small Industries Development Corporation Ltd (SIDCO) in addition to developing infrastructure of industrial estates, plots and sheds, also supplies raw materials like iron and steel, wax, potassium chlorate and printing paper. The office of SIDCO in the industrial estate of Dindugal has now been amalgamated with the Madurai unit. Small Industries Promotion Corporation of Tamilnadu (SIPCOT) has developed an industrial estate at Pallapatti in Nilakottai block which will soon be the site of the proposed Food Park. An Export Oriented Unit (EOU) for fruit and vegetable processing under Agriculture Export Zone (AEZ) for mangoes has come up here. Artisans making brass ware artifacts are concentrated around Nilakottai town. Terra cotta handicrafts are produced by a group of artisans in Dindugal block. Handicraftsmen producing artistic malas worn by devotees inhabit around the religious town of Palani. Beautiful handicrafts, bouquets of dried flowers, toys etc. are produced by artisans around the tourist places of Kodaikanal. More than 2500 families earned their living as artisans.

There are five engineering colleges in the district. There is also one Government run ITI and six private ones. Electrification has reached all the villages in the district. A large number of agro industrial units can be set up in the agro industrial estate established in the district.

The Small Industry Service Institute (SISI) which has ten franchisee centres in the district provides appropriate training in different industrial trades and activities. KVIC at Madurai and KVIB at Dindugal impart 3 day entrepreneurship development training to aspiring Rural Employment Guarantee Programme (REGP) entrepreneurs. The Centre for Entrepreneurship in Gandhigram Rural University (GRU) provides regular entrepreneurship development training to youth in different modern industrial activities. District Industries Centre (DIC) provides Entrepreneurship Development Programme (EDP) training to Prime Misnter's Rozgar Yojana (PMRY) beneficiaries prior to establishment of units. GRU offers post graduate degree in Rural Industrial Management to train managers for industrial units. Vocational training to women entrepreneurs is provided by DIC. Under Swarnajayanthi Gram Swarozgar Yojana (SGSY), training in different industrial trades is provided through NGOs and reputed institutes. There is adequate facility at the district level for testing of water quality for industrial purposes established by the Tamilnadu Water and Drainage Board.

Potentialities of NFS activities in Nagapattinam District

Nagapattinam district is an industrially backward district with 3 blocks viz Sirkali, Kollidam and Keelaiyur declared as "Most Backward" while the remaining 8 blocks declared as "Backward". The agrarian nature of the economy of the district exhibits high level of unemployment and under employment and disguised employment. About 40 percent of the population constitute workers and 60 percent non workers indicating high level of unemployment in the district. The workers also include higher percentage of marginal agricultural labours accounting for 75.73 percent indicating underemployment and disguised employment. (NABARD Nagapattinam District PLCP 2007–08).

At the same time, the agrarian nature of the district offers excellent scope for setting up of agro–based processing units with thrust on pulses, paddy, oil seeds, vegetables, fruits, flowers. Investment credit is a real indicator for the industrial development as it results in creation of capital goods for generation of income and employment.. Investment credit demand for NFS activities in the district can be for the following broad group of activities like Rural Artisans/ Craftsman–Decentralized Sector, Tiny Industries, Cottage and Village industries, Ancillary units, handlooms and Power looms, Agro industries and SSI units.

Infrastructure and economic growth are inter-linked. Inadequate infrastructure severely undermines the growth potential of various sub-sectors of NFS. Besides, sustainability of NFS units/micro enterprises depends on the availability of forward and backward linkages. In a significant move to alter the definition of "village industry" the Government introduced the Khadi and Village Industries Commission (Amendment) Bill 2005, proposing to raise the capital investment ceiling from Rs. 15,000 to Rs. 1 Lakh. This is expected to bring a rise in the number of village industries eligible for assistance by the KVIC and also increase the flow of credit from banks.

Industrial activities in Nagapattinam district are mostly concentrated in Mayiladuthurai and Nagapattinam. The salt based industries are located at Vedharanyam.

The marketing arrangements for most of the NFS products in the district are mostly informal and unorganized, sold within the block/district. Recently some initiatives have been made by District Rural Development Agency (DRDA) to launch a brand name for all the products of micro enterprises by name "Alaimagal". Some of the products of NFS are also put on the web "Rural Bazar" (http://www.ruralbazar.tn.gov.in). As a part of promotional efforts of NABARD, a rural craft mart show casing NFS products have been launched (http://nabard.org/whats/craft/pg/htm).

Classification of Non Farm Sector Activities in Sample Districts

The growth of farm sector is dependent on irrigation system and hence it is location specific. However, NFS could exist and spread breaking geographical barriers. The development of infrastructural facilities is sufficient for the spread of NFS. Hence, it was found in the sample district that NFS activities have been in operational in the districts.

As there is no standard definition for NFS, the list of activities covered under the NFS is not exhaustive. However, for the purpose of providing loans under NFS, NABARD has given list of activities covered under NFS (Annexure – 1). For the purpose of analysis and to identify the potential NFS activities in sample districts, NFS activities are classified on the basis of raw material available, demand in the internal market, skill based export opportunities, types of rural artisans and emerging activities (Chart 3.1).

Chart 3.1

Classification of NFS Activities in Sample Districts

S.No.	Industries	Dindugal District	Nagapattinam District
1.	Raw Material based	Spinning Mill, brick kiln, leather tanning, lock making, brakware industry, food processing, lime stone.	Agro processing activities, horticulture based activities, Cotton textiles, dairy, leather, wood based industries, imitation jewellery etc.
2.	Demand based	Weaving, spinning mill, paper mill, tobacco cigar making, metal industry, dying, iron industry, 'ock units.	Sari weaving, tourism related, readymade garments, fruit processing, brick making , milk chilling and processing etc.

3.	Skill based	Brick kiln, Weaving.	Cotton and silk weaving, brick making etc.
4.	Export oriented	Eucalyptus oil, fruit processing.	Herbal products, Fruit process, organic fruits etc.
5.	Rural Artisans	Pottery, Paper making, toys making, terra cotta.	Small trade and petty shops, dairy products, service activities, village industry, fish processing.
6.	Emerging activities	Building materials and Ceramics.	Building material, packaging material and packaging activities, aromatic oil making, etc.

Business Policies and Performance of PCARDBs with Special Reference to NFS Loans

Though the basic objective of PCARDBs was to fund for long term operations on land, the introduction of NFS loan are the result of adaptive strategy followed by PCARDBs. Adaptive strategy, which implies that "the development of a viable match between the opportunities and the risks present in the external environment and the organization's capabilities and resources for exploiting these opportunities". There has always been a correlation between agricultural growth and NFS (NABARD). Both the negative and positive growth of the former will affect the latter. An additional income in the NFS naturally will boost the investments in farm sector. It has been found during discussions with the bank officials that the income earned through NFS has made the "land less" as "land lords". Because owning a farmland in a village is a matter of prestige for an average Tamilnadu villager.

On the other hand, when an average farmer gets surplus income from agriculture naturally he intends to invest in NFS. One or more of the following propositions are the reasons for this investment. *a)* the input for the majority of the NFS is contributed by the agriculture sector; *b)* an average farmer lacks knowledge on the economic activities which are too away from the purview of his traditional occupation; *c)* farmers' apathy to move away from his native land. Also, when there is a failure in the farm business an enterprising farmer seeks shelter in NFS for his daily bread.

His education, rural infrastructure, rural finance (Peter Lanjouw : 1998), process of urbanization (Kundu : 1991) or social status, savings (Banerjee : 1997) may influence him to undertake NFS. Among these factors the role of finance has special significance. Without institutional finance the growth and spread of NFS will become questionable. In this direction, NABARD has created a separate Department to look after the development of NFS in the country. Policy formulation, monitoring and providing refinance to the institutional agencies for financing to NFS have become one of the key areas before NABARD. In these contexts this chapter reviews the flow of finance to NFS at different level as well as at sample PCARDBs level.

Progress in NFS Loan Operations at National Level

Agency-wise flow of refinance for NFS

To analyze the progress of NFS loans operations at national level the refinance provided by NABARD to various institutional agencies has been taken for analysis, because at institutional level classified data especially for NFS were not readily available. NABARD provide refinance facility to all institutional agencies, viz., Commercial Bank (CB), RRB, State Cooperative Bank (SCB) and State Cooperative Agriculture Rural Development Banks (SCARDBs) for providing loans to NFS.

Table 3.1

Agency-wise Flow of Refinance under NFS (Investment Credit) All India Level

(Rs. in Crores)

Years	*CBs*	*SCARDB*	*SCB*	*RRB*	*Scheduled PUCBs*	*Total*
2001-02	386.11	462.69	347.54	356.32	63.31	1615.97
	(23.89)	(28.63)	(21.50)	(22.04)	(3.91)	(100)
2002-03	160.00	551.10	768.36	527.00	0.94	2007.40
	(7.97)	(27.45)	(38.26)	(26.25)	(0.04)	(100)
2003-04	414.92	501.26	827.25	598.34	21.44	2363.22
	(17.56)	(21.21)	(35.00)	(25.32)	(0.91)	(100)

2004-05	531.40 (20.90)	623.61 (24.53)	625.81 (24.61)	756.86 (29.77)	4.89 (0.19)	2542.58 (100)
2005-06	699.77 (30.61)	589.72 (25.80)	533.13 (23.32)	457.40 (20.25)	5.96 (0.26)	2285.98 (100)

Source: Data compiled from reports of the NABARD for various years.

Note: Figure in Parenthesis indicate the percentage to respective total.

Diagram 3.1

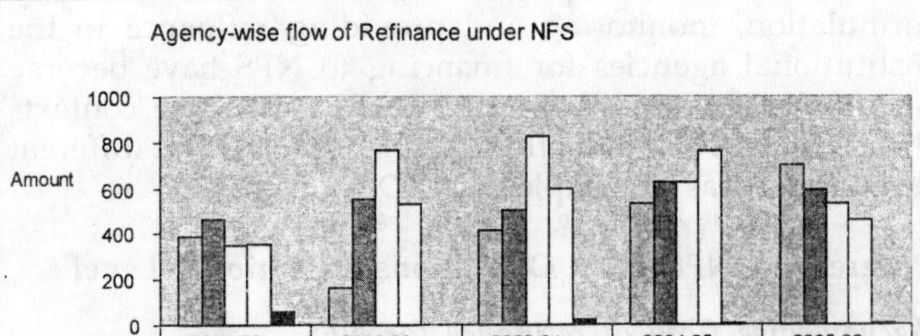

	2001-02	2002-03	2003-04	2004-05	2005-06
CBs	386.11	160.01	414.92	531.4	699.77
SCARDBs	462.69	551.1	501.26	623.61	589.72
SCBs	347.54	768.36	827.25	625.81	533.13
RRBs	356.32	527	598.34	756.86	457.4
PUCBs	63.31	0.94	21.44	4.89	5.96

Year

The agency wise analysis shows that SCARDB holds major share in NABARD refinance during the year 2001-02 whereas, CBs dominated the scene during 2005-06 at all India level. In the case of Tamilnadu the State Cooperative Bank availed more refinance under this scheme from NABARD. As the NABARD's refinance is linked with recovery level, the poor recovery at Agricultural Rural Development Banks (ARDBs) level affected their eligibility for refinance. Hence the shares of SCARDBs have come down over the years.

Region Wise Flow of Refinance Under NFS

The country has been divided in to six regions for purposes of providing refinance for NFS. They are Northern Region, Northeast Region, East Region, Central Region, West Region and South Region. The region wise refinance under NFS is analyzed in the table 3.2.

Table 3.2: Region-Wise Flow of Refinance Under NFS (Investment Credit) All India Level

(Rs.in Crores)

Year	*North Region*	*North East Region*	*East Region*	*Central Region*	*West Region*	*South Region*	*Total*
2001-2002	248.51 (15.37)	56.77 (3.51)	376.46 (23.79)	100.71 (6.21)	220.69 (13.65)	612.83 (37.92)	1615.97 (100)
2002-2003	364.04 (18.10)	98.63 (5.00)	419.95 (21.00)	264.77 (13.20)	116.88 (5.80)	743.13 (37.01)	2007.40 (100)
2003-2004	445.31 (18.80)	106.30 (4.50)	537.10 (22.60)	304.93 (13.00)	276.27 (11.71)	693.91 (29.40)	2363.22 (100)
2004-2005	618.01 (24.31)	193.73 (7.62)	480.90 (18.91)	293.70 (11.55)	222.47 (8.75)	733.77 (28.86)	2542.58 (100)
2005-2006	599.26 (26.21)	98.25 (4.30)	594.68 (26.01)	329.84 (14.43)	213.92 (9.36)	450.03 (19.68)	2285.97 (100)

Source: Data compiled from reports of the NABARD for various years.

Note: Figure in Parenthesis indicate the percentage to respective total.

Diagram 3.2

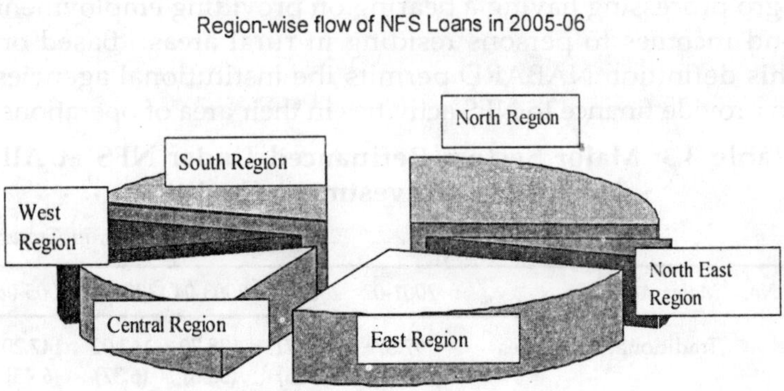

The Regional wise analysis shows that the Southern Region which consists of Andrapredesh, Karnataka, Kerala, Pondichery, Lakshadweep and Tamilnadu availed more refinance compared to other regions in India upto the year 2004 - 05. The Northern Region which consists of

Chandigarh, New Delhi, Haryana, Himachal Pradesh, Jammu and Kashmir, Punjab and Rajasthan availed more refinance under NFS during the year 2005-06 followed by East region. This trend revealed that NFS as a breeder of employment opportunity had attracted the attention of people across the country.

Major Sectors Refinance Under NFS at All India Level

As discussed already there is no standard definition for NFS, either internationally or within India. The sector is too diverse, in terms of activities, unit sizes and geographic dispersal. This is further emphasized by the fact that the sector is usually defined in negative terms as the rural non-farm or non-agricultural sector. Positive terms, such as rural enterprises or rural industries are inadequate. Hence, NABARD has redefined NFS as those enterprises and artisanal activities which could be classified as household, decentralized, tiny and small scale enterprises involved in production/ manufacturing, processing, preserving, storing and marketing of goods and /or engaged in services and agro processing having a bearing on providing employment and incomes to persons residing in rural areas. Based on this definition NABARD permits the institutional agencies to provide finance to NFS activities in their area of operations.

Table 3.3: Major Sectors Refinanced Under NFS at All India Level (Investment Credit)

(Rs. in Crores)

S.No.	*Major Activities*	*2001-02*	*2002-03*	*2003-04*	*2004-05*	*2005-06*
1.	Traditional Industries	97.57 (6.03)	125.71 (6.26)	138.70 (5.86)	162.02 (6.37)	147.20 (6.43)
2.	Agro–process/Agro Inds.	82.85 (5.12)	95.95 (4.77)	73.23 (3.09)	47.40 (1.86)	80.76 (3.53)
3.	Handicrafts	20.72 (1.28)	42.97 (2.14)	29.01 (1.22)	30.03 (1.18)	29.61 (1.29)
4.	Handlooms	09.52 (0.58)	8.49 (0.42)	13.89 (0.58)	12.60 (0.49)	14.81 (0.64)
5.	Engineering Industries	41.99 (2.59)	62.76 (3.12)	69.84 (2.95)	72.69 (2.85)	15.07 (0.65)

6.	Bldg/Const. Materials	47.14 (2.91)	40.11 (1.99)	26.35 (1.11)	33.90 (1.33)	15.89 (0.69)
7.	Modern activities	55.59 (3.44)	135.60 (6.75)	91.82 (3.88)	99.03 (3.89)	68.87 (3.01)
8.	Transport Vehicles	213.93 (13.23)	134.05 (6.67)	110.55 (4.67)	119.00 (4.68)	95.83 (4.19)
9.	Service Activities	234.93 (14.51)	245.86 (12.24)	267.52 (11.32)	286.16 (11.25)	280.69 (12.27)
10.	Rural Housing	501.88 (31.05)	769.53 (38.33)	1030.23 (43.59)	1276.94 (50.22)	1242.80 (54.36)
11.	Other Misc.	310.20 (19.19)	346.38 (17.25)	512.07 (21.66)	402.82 (15.84)	294.45 (12.88)
	Total	1615.97	2007.40	2363.22	2542.58	2285.98

Source: Data compiled from reports of the NABARD for various years.

Note: Figure in Parenthesis indicate the percentage to respective total.

Diagram 3.3

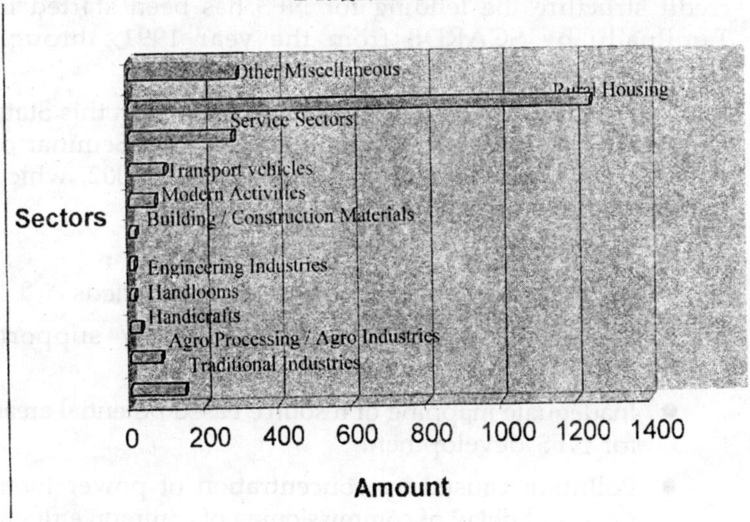

It could be understood from the table that at the national level the major sectors, which attracted refinance during the past from NABARD are:

1) Traditional Industries
2) Agro Processing / Agro Industries
3) Handicrafts

4) Handlooms
5) Engineering Industries
6) Building / Construction Materials
7) Modern Activities
8) Transport Vehicles
9) Service Activities
10) Rural Housing
11) Other Miscellaneous sectors.

The table further reveals that a major segment of refinance was given for rural housing followed by other miscellaneous activities, service activities and transport vehicles in that order in all the years under study.

Progress in NFS loan operations at Tamilnadu Level

In Tamilnadu both the short term and long term credit structure provide loans for NFS. In the case of long term credit structure the lending for NFS has been started in Tamilnadu by SCARDB from the year 1991, through PCARDBs.

The constraints for the slow growth of NFS in this State is listed in the Report of the State Level Credit Seminar of NABARD held at Chennai on 22nd January 2002, which holds good even today, are;

- Frequent interruption in power supply.
- Inadequate number of common work sheds.
- Inadequate marketing infrastructure / support, especially for handicrafts products
- Inadequate mapping of resource based potential areas for NFS development
- Pollution caused by concentration of power loom units and delay of commissioning of common effluent treatment plans
- Lack of effective coordination among promotional, regulatory and financial institutions
- Inadequate / absence of timely credit flow to the sector, leading to cost over runs

Table 3.4: Non–Farm Sector Loan Issued at PCARDB Level in Tamilnadu

(Rs. in Crores)

Year	*Total Loan*	*NFS*	*% Share*
2000-01	20093.43	5573.26	27.73
2001-02	19240.51 (- 4.24)	5321.65 (-4.51)	27.65
2002-03	21791.62 (13.25)	5909.37 (11.04)	27.11
2003-04	12700.25 (- 4171)	2618.88 (-55.68)	20.62
2004-05	1243.96 (-90.20)	115.53 (-95.58)	9.28

Source: Data compiled from records maintained by TNSCARDB for various years.

Note: Figures in Parenthesis indicates the percentage changes.

Diagram 3.4

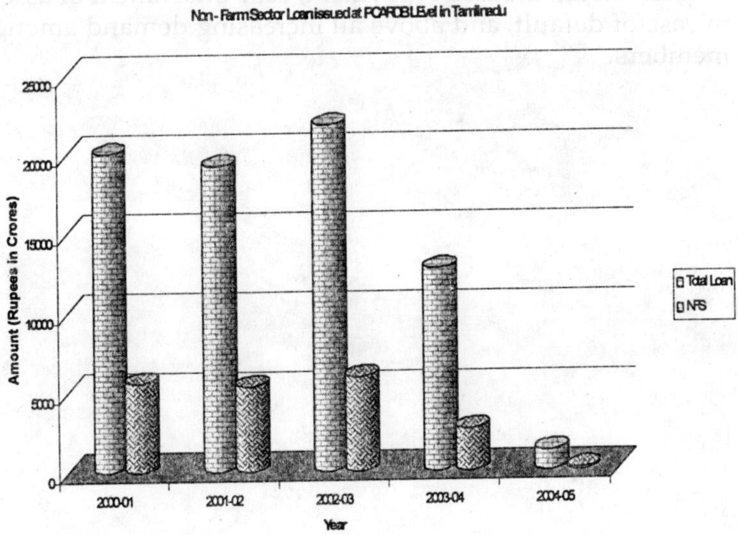

The available figure shows that NFS did not receive much attention. At the State level it was found that the total agricultural loans issued by PCARDBs in Tamilnadu have increased from Rs. 20093.43 crores to Rs.21791.62 crores during the period 2000-01 to 2002-03. The total NFS loans issued by PCARDBs have increased from Rs.5573.26 crores to 5909.37 crores during the same period. Thereafter the total agricultural loan as well as NFS loan issued has come down heavily and the percentage of NFS loans in the total loans has come down to 9.28 from 27 per cent during the year 2000-01. This shows that NFS have not received due recognition.

NFS Loan in Dindugal District

It was found that all categories of loans were issued by PCARDBs in Dindugal district under NFS. They are namely Composite Loans, Integrated Loans, Small Road Transport Operations (SRTO) Loans and other Loans. Invariably all the sample banks have issued more loans for SRTO, because of clear title, easy procedure, bankable return on investment comparatively higher than other NFS activities (as perceived by borrowers), assured repayment, easy attachment of asset in case of default, and above all increasing demand among members.

Table 3.5: NFS Loan Issued in Dindugal District

(Rs.in lakhs)

Year	Dindugal		Kodaikanal		Oddanchattram		Palani		Reddiarchatram		Vedesanthur		Total	
	NFS	Total	NFS	Total	NFS	Total	NFS	Total	NFS	Total	NFS	Total	NFS	Total
2001-02	19.96	80.34	1.69	53.23	0.80	90.99	21.13	150.94	3.57	93.13	14.02	153.03	61.17	621.66
	(24.84)	(100)	(3.17)	(100)	(0.87)	(100)	(13.99)	(100)	(38.33)	(100)	(9.16)	(100)	(9.83)	(100)
2002-03	11.97	126.22	3.84	54.40	3.92	96.91	17.67	126.33	5.52	101.05	31.43	173.32	74.35	678.23
	(9.48)	(100)	(7.06)	(100)	(4.04)	(100)	(13.98)	(100)	(5.46)	(100)	(18.13)	(100)	(10.96)	(100)
2003-04	4.25	80.44	2.91	32.45	4.59	28.22	14.88	73.38	2.05	63.55	16.38	59.78	45.06	337.82
	(5.28)	(100)	(8.96)	(100)	(16.26)	(100)	(20.27)	(100)	(3.22)	(100)	(27.40)	(100)	(13.33)	(100)
2004-05	DNA	3.31	DNA	DNA	0.61	6.51	3.66	17.21	DNA	10.88	0.70	14.59	4.97	52.50
		(100)			(9.37)	(100)	(21.26)	(100)		(100)	(4.79)	(100)	(9.46)	(100)
2005-06	DNA	DNA	DNA	DNA	DNA	DNA	DNA	DNA	DNA	DNA	DNA	DNA	DNA	DNA

Source: Complied from Annual and Audit Reports for various years.

Note: Figures in Parenthesis indicates the percentage to respective total

DNA–Data Not Available

Diagram 3.5

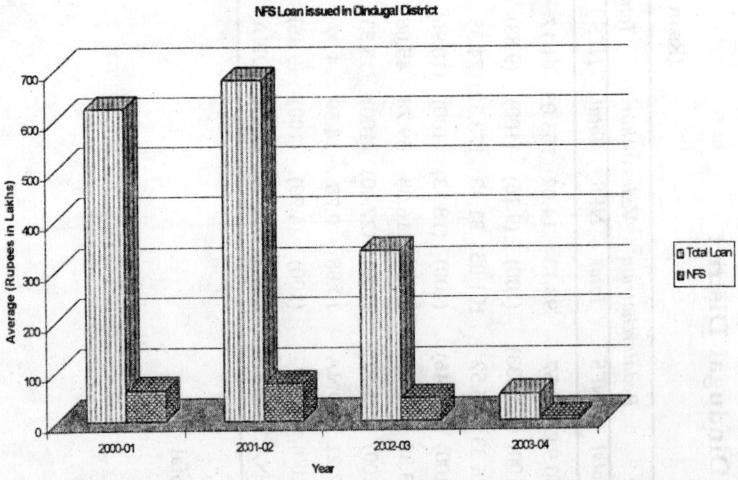

In Dindugal district it is evident that the NFS loans issued by all the six PCARDBs were not an encouraging one. In Dindugal and Reddiyarchathiram PCARDB it was on the decreasing order during study period. In Kodaikannal and in Palani it was on the increasing order. However the NFS in Kodaikannal was less than 10 percent of the total loan and in Palani it was less than 22 percent. In Oddanchatram also the same poor state of affairs could be seen. In Vedasandur the NFS loan was on the increasing order till 2003 – 04 and there was a steep fall in the year 2004 – 05.

It is to be noted here that the changed scenario in the political setup of Tamilnadu which wrote off the dues of entire past loan made PCARDBs to a stand still. Neither agriculture loans nor NFS loans issued during the year 2005–06 data were not available for that particular year. A study on the total loan of the district reveal that the maximum quantum of loan issued for the NFS was in the year 2003 – 04 which was only 13.33 percent of the total loan.

NFS Loan in Nagapattinam District

Though Nagapattinam district when compared to Dindugal district is an agriculturally developed one, the NFS activities are flourishing equally here. May be due to the agricultural potentiality the NFS activities are limited, but the share of loan by PCARDBs is comparatively high in this district.

Table 3.6: NFS Loan Issued in Nagapattinam District

(Rs.in lakhs)

Years	*Mayiladuthurai PCARDB*		*Sirkali PCARDB*		*Vedaranyam PCARDB*		*Total*	
Loans	*NFS*	*Total*	*NFS*	*Total*	*NFS*	*Total*	*NFS*	*Total*
2001-02	85.28 (38.17)	223.39 (100)	28.62 (6.04)	473.59 (100)	74.63 (47.35)	157.59 (100)	188.53 (22.06)	854.57 (100)
2002-03	94.05 (52.09)	180.54 (100)	44.03 (8.44)	521.49 (100)	79.15 (39.18)	202.01 (100)	217.23 (24.02)	904.04 (100)
2003-04	21.02 (52.92)	39.72 (100)	75.83 (13.83)	548.14 (100)	81.38 (34.55)	235.49 (100)	178.23 (21.64)	823.35 (100)
2004-05	3.11 (29.33)	10.60 (100)	81.82 (16.06)	509.15 (100)	73.73 (35.51)	207.58 (100)	158.66 (21.81)	727.33 (100)
2005-06	0.10 (6.25)	1.60 (100)	51.31 (11.17)	459.00 (100)	66.24 (35.57)	186.18 (100)	117.65 (18.19)	646.78 (100)

Source: Complied from Annual and Audit Reports of sample banks for various years.

Note: Figures in Parenthesis indicates the percentage to respective total.

Diagram 3.6

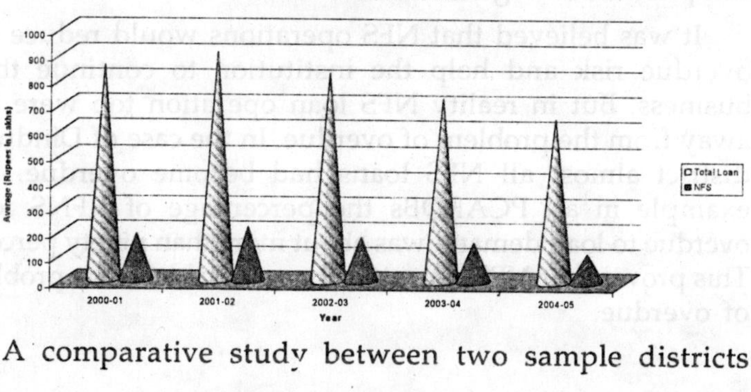

A comparative study between two sample districts

reveals that the NFS activities in Nagapattinam district were better than its counterpart. In Mayiladuthurai out of the total loan issued the share of NFS loans was to the extent of 38.17 percent , 52.09 percent, 52.92 percent, 29.33 percent and 6.25 percent during the years 2001 – 02 to 2005 – 06 respectively. However the other two PCARDBs in the district namely Sirkali and Vedharanyam the picture of the NFS loan was not as rosy as that of Mayiladuthurai. It was less than 48 percent of loan in Vedharanyam and less than 14 percent in Sirkali in all the years under study. The study of total loans of the district, because of the pulling down of Vedharanyam and Sirkali PCARDBs, the NFS loan was less than 25 percent during the entire period of study.

Position of overdue in NFS loans in sample district

Overdue is a perennial problem in all the PCARDBs in Tamilnadu. The waiving of loans and interest, by the governments every now and then gives strong impressions in the minds of agriculturists and other members who obtained loans from PCARDBs to become a defaulter. The PCARDBs are also not in a position to take any stringent measures in recovering such loans because of political pressures. The dismissal of elected board often by the elected governments, and appointment of Special Officers make the problem more complex one. Without looking into the records of any PCARDBs, one can easily say that a particular PCARDB has overdue problem. However to make a detailed study on this overdue position in the sample district the compiled data is given below.

It was believed that NFS operations would reduce the overdue risk and help the institution to continue their business. But in reality NFS loan operation too were not away from the problem of overdue. In the case of Dindugal district almost all NFS loans had become overdue. For example in all PCARDBs the percentage of RFNS loan overdue to loan demand was about more than ninety percent. This proves that NFS loans too are vulnerable to the problem of overdue.

Table 3.7

Position of Demand and Balance in NFS Loan Operation – Dindugal District

(Rs. Lakhs)

S. No.	*Name of the PCARD Bank*	*2001–2002*		*2002–2003*		*2003–2004*		*2004–2005*		*2005–2006*	
		Demand	*Overdue*	*Demand*	*Overdue*	*Demand*	*Overdue*	*Demand*	*Overdue*	*Demand*	*Overdue*
	Dindugal	44.65 (100)	26.47 (59.3)	36.18 (100)	25.18 (69.6)	41.38 (100)	30.00 (72.5)	41.54 (100)	39.34 (94.8)	51.25 (100)	45.84 (89.4)
	Kodaikanal	35.13 (100)	29.19 (83.0)	35.07 (100)	27.27 (77.7)	30.37 (100)	27.75 (91.4)	33.97 (100)	31.68 (93.2)	31.93 (100)	30.83 (96.5)
	Oddanchatram	23.94 (100)	18.68 (28.0)	16.83 (100)	13.30 (79.0)	21.72 (100)	19.38 (89.2)	30.95 (100)	27.03 (87.3)	31.40 (100)	29.06 (92.5)
	Palani	36.94 (100)	26.90 (73.0)	37.66 (100)	27.07 (71.9)	41.82 (100)	32.72 (78.2)	49.30 (100)	43.93 (89.1)	44.13 (100)	35.00 (79.3)
	Reddiarchatram	13.20 (100)	6.25 (47.0)	7.02 (100)	3.82 (54.4)	5.55 (100)	4.18 (75.3)	6.49 (100)	4.67 (72.0)	7.11 (100)	6.44 (90.5)
	Vedasandur	37.19 (100)	26.11 (70.0)	32.91 (100)	29.70 (90.2)	46.04 (100)	40.31 (87.5)	57.83 (100)	53.00 (91.6)	73.41 (100)	70.88 (96.5)

Source: Complied from Annual and Audit Reports for various years.
Note : Figures in Parenthesis indicates the percentage of Overdue to Demand

Table 3.8

Position of Demand and Overdue in NFS Loan Operation – Nagapattinam District

(Rs. lakhs)

S. No.	Name of the PCARD Bank	2001–2002		2002–2003		2003–2004		2004–2005		2005–2006	
		Demand	Overdue	Demand	Overdue	Demand	Overdue	Demand	Overdue	Demand	Overdue
	Mayiladuthurai	155.87	82.53	217.40	88.60	204.54	109.52	202.56	127.06	184.27	131.38
			(53.0)		(40.7)		(53.5)		(62.7)		(71.3)
	Sirkali	66.21	43.43	86.23	48.98	94.45	54.69	101.26	63.73	30.11	29.16
			(65.6)		(56.8)		(58.0)		(63.0)		(96.8)
	Vedharanyam	64.83	25.75	77.42	32.85	109.77	41.92	106.10	63.14	122.91	55.19
			(40.0)		(42.4)		(38.2)		(59.5)		(45.0)

Source: Complied from Annual and Audit Reports for various years.

Note : Figures in Parenthesis indicates the percentage of Overdue to Demand.

It was found from the study that in Nagapattinam district 52.8 percent of the NFS loan demand was overdue in 2001–02, which has increased to 64 percent in 2005–06. The individual bank wise analysis shows that the problem was serious in Sirkali PCARDB, where more than 96 percent of the NFS loan demand was loan overdue.

Perception on the NFS Loan Operations

Members who wanted to get NFS loan from PCARDBs have to submit loan application in the form prescribed for the required purpose, with documents listed in the box 3.1.

A detailed assessment of the value of the land is the critical work, while processing the loan application. After getting legal opinion, the bank officials viz: Land Valuation Officers, and the technical supervisor inspect the land offered as security and the development proposal for determining the economic viability and technical feasibility of the scheme. From November 1971 onwards, a uniform method of valuation of the land is adopted. Ordinarily 50 percent of the total land value of Sub Registrar Office guidelines is treated as eligibility for the loan amount.

Box 3.1

List of Loan Documents

1. Current Cropping pattern	
2. Copy of Adangal	
3. Land area Sketch	
4. A Certificate for showing the member is not defaulted for any government loan/tax	Obtained from Revenue Department
5. Encumbrance certificate for land offered as security for 13 years.	
6. A certificate from Commercial bank	Showing the member is not a defaulter
7. A certificate from PACB	

8. Quotation for machinery to be purchased from authorized dealers	To access the viability of the project and to as certain the genuine of the machinery
9. Other documents demanded by PCARDBs concerned	To strengthen the viability of borrowers interest in loan.

With a view to identify the perception of the stake holders– members and the employees on the approaches of PCARDBs in NFS loan operations, Participatory Rural Appraisal (PRA) techniques such as Problem Identification and Prioritization, and Focus Group Discussions (FGD) were used. These exercises were conducted separately among different groups of members and the employees in the sample districts. A summary of the inferences of these exercises is given in the box 3.2.

Box 3.2

Problems in NFS loan operations

Sl. No.	*Perception of Borrowers*	*Perception of Employees*
1	Defective asset valuation norms and procedures	Identification of potential borrowers
2	Time consuming procedures	Burden of loans because of multi agency credit
3	High cost of borrowings	Target approach in lending
4	Delay in loan sanction	Absence of democratic governance
5	Loans are not available as and when it is required	Interferences of pressure groups

Source: Compiled from FGD conducted among sample respondents and Employees of PCARDBs in the sample districts during different occasions.

Perception of the Borrowers

During the PRA exercises among sample respondents it was found that :

(1) Defective asset valuation norms and procedures
(2) Time consuming procedures
(3) High cost of borrowing
(4) Delay in loan sanction and
(5) Loans are not available as and when it is required.

Were the problems perceived by the borrowers of NFS loans.

Defective Asset Valuation Norms and Procedure

The first problem raised by the sample respondents was the defective asset valuation norms and procedures. For issuing loans PCARDBs hypothecate the assets of the borrowers and the repaying capacity of the borrower is fixed based on the value of the assets especially landed properties. The respondents in both the sample districts opined that the asset valuation norms adopted by the PCARDBs are absolute and decrease the repaying capacity of the borrower.

Time Consuming Procedures

The next rank goes to the problems associated with loan procedures. The sample respondents opined that the procedures followed by PCARDBs were time consuming and traditional. Unnecessarily the productive times of employees and members were wasted. As per the procedure, every loan application must be processed and loan must be sanctioned within 28 days from the date of submission of the loan application, provided the application was technically correct. But getting certificates from the revenue authorities, registration of documents, contribution to share capital, and other procedures adversely consume much time and cause inordinate delay in sanctioning loan.

High Cost of Borrowings

The third problem was cost of borrowings. During case analysis it is computed that cost of borrowing forms nearly 6.8 per cent plus down payment (10 percent) plus share capital (5 percent). Further, as PCARDBs cover larger area of operation, the cost of transport and other incidental chargers incurred by the borrowers increase the cost of borrowers.

Delay in Loan Sanction

The next important problem envisaged by the sample respondents was delay in sanctioning of loan. During discussion, it was noticed that the delay in loan was due to lengthy loaning procedure and targeted lending. It means, the PCARDBs collect the loan applications till January-February months and process the same before the end of the financial year. The delay in loan was also caused due to delay in scrutiny of the application by the bank and calling for clarifications/ratifications. The other problems, which the borrower envisaged were arbitrary scale of finance, security oriented lending policies and defective recovery practices. The cost escalation due to abnormal lead time, absence of micro level planning in preparing scale of finance, absence of pledge and hypothecation loans etc., also were felt by the sample respondents.

Loans are not available as and when it is required

One of the major problems in NFS, activities for sample respondents was non-availability of working capital. The sample respondents felt that even after the emergence of new generation banks, PCARDBs were unable to meet the additional demand of borrowers, as and when it is required.

Employee's Perception on NFS Loan Operations

How do the employees perceive the NFS loan operations? It is ultimately they who play a major role to make the scheme success or failure. The employees though endorsed the problems perceived by the members, added some more problems associated in NFS lending and recovery.

Identification of Potential Entrepreneurs

This problem gets compounded due to targeted lending

coupled with lack of viable projects. The banks need entrepreneurial investors who can be a stakeholder for the resources of banks. Hence, at present the repayment culture of the borrower is considered more important than the technical feasibility of the project for which the borrower demands credit. That is the reason why, major attention is given for SRTO loans. It is found that nearly 44 per cent of the members found to be borrowers of SRTO loans from the sample banks in the both districts. However more than 2/3 of them were one-time borrowers. Moreover `agency shift' is visible, i.e., members exit from their own cooperatives and seek shelter in other rural financial institutions. This trend causes concern among the bankers. Because in future due to 'targeted lending approach' unavailable projects and non-credit worthy members may become part of the system. This would affect the banking system.

Burden of Loan because of Multi Agency Credit

It was revealed that multi agency approach in rural credit had aggravated debt burden among people. Borrowers were tempted to borrow more funds from more than one agency by adopting unfair practices. Differences in policies and procedures among organized financing institutions also helped borrowers in availing financial assistances from more than one agency.

Target Approach in Lending

The targets were fixed by State Government and SCARDB and assigned for execution by PCARDBs. Because of this pressure the PCARDBs is sanctioning loan for unviable projects also. Some times more loans are sanctioned for the existing borrowers. Further, the disbursement of NFS loans start in a year after January and the bank is urged to achieve the target on or before 31st March every year. This time constraint leads to various lacuna in sanctioning loan.

Absence of Democratic Governance

Democratic governance is one of the characteristics of a cooperative management and it reflects cooperatives' distinguished quality. The four key components of cooperative governance are accountability, transparency, consistency and participation. The elected body of cooperative organization is often dismissed and the administration is entrusted with a single man, with the designation of Special Officers. Normally the Special Officer is a foreigner to the area, unable to judge the background of borrowers. On the basis of the paper presented only, the Spcial Officers sanctions loans and the integrity of the borrowers are not tested. Hence the recovery of loans from such borrowers becomes difficult.

Command of Pressure Groups

There seems to be a close nexus between cooperatives and pressure groups. PCARDBs were not exception to the rule. Absence of dedicated cooperative leaders and the lake of commitment among stakeholders, paved way for pressure groups to use PCARDBs for their personal and political gains.

The foregoing analysis indicate that the problems associated with designing the NFS lending seem to have caused by the factors, which are beyond the purview of PCARDBs. They warrant policy interventions.

Conclusion

It is also found that both the Centre and State Governments started to realize the significance of NFS due to its role in changing economic development. Among other things the development of NFS largely depends upon the availability of credit facilities. PCARDBs, which have identified NFS as a viable area for diversification, have yet to harvest the opportunities both at State and at Primary level. The NFS loan operations at PCARDBs level showed that NFS loan was meant only for SRTO, neglecting the potential of other areas. It is high time that the potentiality of NFS must be realized and harvested early by PCARDBs otherwise new players will enter into NFS market. Hence, the present approach in NFS lending need to be redesigned as user-friendly. On the other hand, the problem of overdue is a burden to banks. Because of this trend, there was probability of every new loan become overdue and every new borrower becomes defaulter to banks. The trend was even worse when there existed chances for overdue become NPA. Because of this trend the PCARDBs should concentrate on disbursement of NFS loan, so as to balance the situation. It needs policy interventions.

4

The Role of NFS in Employment Generation and Poverty Reduction

The access to credit by the poor in South Asia has been recognized as one of the crucial factors in the alleviation of rural poverty (Human Development in South Asia: 2002, p. 89).. In India, since the introduction of the first Cooperative Credit Societies Act 1904 and the nationalization of CBs in 1969, various schemes and programmes of the Government developed institutional infrastructure which, in turn, resulted in the creation of massive network for rural banking. Sizeable numbers of rural households are, however, away from the purview of the institutional sources. Access to institutional credit is a major indicator, which decides the productivity of rural households and spread NFS. Social scientists have been paying much importance to the problems associated with access to credit for NFS.

The World Bank, National Council for Applied Economic Research (NCAER) Rural Financial Access Survery of 2003 clearly confirmed that access to the formal financial institutions remained severely constrained in rural areas, particularly for the poorest of the households, with informal lending still remaining substantial (Priya Basu, Pradeep Srivastave: 2005, p. 1747). If access to credit is made easy when it is required, half the problems in the NFS could be solved. But the problems pertaining to the access remains complex and deeper than what is generally perceived. Both the institutional and individual factors decide the accessibility to institutional credit. The institutional factors are: the Type of the bank, Location, Experience of bank in NFS lending, Procedures followed, Transaction Cost involved, Amount of Loan available and its Interest, Perception of the Employees on NFS activities etc. The Individuals factors are the demographic, social and economic profile of the individuals, their relationship with the bank, perception of individuals on the functioning of the bank etc. The present study primarily aims at unearthing the factors at the borrowers level, contributing or otherwise to the access to PCARDBs credit for NFS. It also tries to reveal the role of NFS in Employment Generation and Poverty Reduction in sample districts. This analysis is primarily based on opinions of the sample respondents. There is no approved statistics on the role of NFS in employment generation at field level. Keeping this in mind, the researcher has taken diligent care to analyze the response of the respondents.

Demographic, Social and Economic Profiles of the Respondents

Identifying the demographic characteristics of the respondents as well as their socio-economic background would, in turn, help to fix the borrower households on the social ladder of the area under study. The researcher would then be in a position to establish the relationship between the demographic socio-economic variables and NFS in the study area. All the demographic, social and economic variable can be classified into two sets. The first set of variables is called 'ascriptive', which includes caste, kinship relationships, family relationships, occupation, income etc. The other set is the 'achieved' which encompasses the individual attainment through the efforts like education, occupational skills, economic returns etc. In addition to these two sets of variables, the 'life experiences' of an individual also influence his or her attitude and behaviour pattern (Savitha

Thakur Joshi: 1999, p. 8). Coupled with the 'life experience factor', the 'ascriptive' and 'achieved' variables would get transferred into socio-economic variables and help to determine the social and economic status of the borrowers in the community.

Sex

Development literature differentiates sex from gender. Sex relates to the biological differences between male and female. Gender relates to the roles of male and female in the society. The PCARDBs may not formally indulge in sex discrimination against women for the purpose of extending loan, but, there may be a number of formalities, which a loanee has to complete. Further, while advancing loans, the PCARDBs may also demand surety or guarantee, which in the villages is primarily based on land. As family lands are in the name of the male members, women are further put to disadvantageous position (Human Development in South Asia: 2002, pp. 114-155).

Table 4.1

Sex-wise Distribution of Respondents in Sample Districts

Sex	*Dindugal*	*Nagapattinam*	*Total*
Male	303 (86.1)	231 (88.2)	534 (67)
Female	49 (13.9)	31 (11.8)	80 (13)
Total	352 (100)	262 (100)	614 (100)

Source: Data compiled from respondents schedule.

Note: Figures in brackets are percentage to respective total

The study found that 87 per cent of the respondent of the study were male. The district wise analysis shows no much difference. The number of women respondent represented in the sample was very poor. As there is a lot of scope for the promotion of NFS among the women the bankers should concentrate in this area.

Age

Age as an important demographic variable, which not only determines an individual's physical and mental maturity but also depicts his or her life experiences. It decides the participation of the individual in the affairs of the rural credit institutions. There is close relationship between age and member's participation in cooperatives (Pattarnaraka K. 2003, p.265). While studies have attempted to prove that age influenced the repayment behaviour and ethics of the respondents (Sivaprakasam P : 1993, p.46 and Joy Joseph Puthussery: 1999, p.9), the other studies proved contra (Chidambaram K. et.al., 1999, p.4).

Those persons who have completed 18 years of age and competent to contract are eligible to become members of PCARDB as per Sec. 21 of the Tamil Nadu State Cooperative Societies Act 1983.

Table 4.2

Age-wise distribution of Respondents in Sample Districts

Age	*Dindugal*	*Nagapattinam*	*Total*
>35	10(2.8)	18(6.9)	28(4.7)
36-50	81(23.0)	151(57.6)	232(37.7)
<50	261(74.2)	93(35.5)	354(57.6)
Total	352(100)	262(100)	614(100)

Source : Data compiled from respondents schedule.

Note: Figures in brackets are percentage to respective total.

It was found that across the state, the participation of younger generation is less in the affairs of cooperatives as the boards of cooperative societies have been superseded and the opportunity for democratic management is negated for cooperative societies in Tamilnadu. In this study also it was found that in Dindugal district majority of the respondents belonged to the category of more than 50 years of age. Contradictory to this trend, majority of the respondents in Nagapattinam District belonged to the age group of 36-50. In both the districts the participation of the younger generation i.e., the respondents belonged to the age group of less than 35, was poor.

Community

The Indian society has been stratified on the basis of community especially in rural areas. Community is perceived as an important factor, which determines one's social prestige and social intercourse.

Members are not discriminated based on caste, community, religion, sex, colour and race etc. in the cooperative society. In fact the basic approach for cooperative movement in 1904 was to protect the interest of the weaker sections from the unfair trading practices of the money lenders, middle men and village traders. Thereafter during planning period also the Government of India used cooperatives as a vehicle for the socio-economic development of the weaker sections. The Government of Tamil Nadu has given provisions of the Tamil Nadu Cooperative Societies Act and Rules to include the weaker sections in the board management of the cooperative enterprises.

Table 4.3

Community-wise Distribution of Respondents in Sample Districts

Community	*Dindugal*	*Nagapattinam*	*Total*
SC	32(9.1)	19(7.2)	51(8.3)
MBC & BC	286(81.2)	212(80.9)	498(81.1)
OC	34(9.7)	31(11.9)	65(10.6)
Total	352(100)	262(100)	614(100)

Source: Data compiled from respondents schedule.

Note: Figures in brackets are percentage to respective total.

The study found that majority of the respondent in both the regions belonged to MBC and BC. Only 8.3 percent of the sample respondents belonged to weaker sections. It was found that labour migration was the major reason among these communities for not availing loans for NFS activities. The promotion of NFS among the weaker sections could be able to arrest the problem of labour migration by way of increasing the employment opportunities as well as the income.

Educational Status

Education not only widens the knowledge but also helps a person to make use of rational and scientific approach to solve problems. The educated borrowers have the tendency to utilize their loans on productive and specified purpose (Debrata Das: 2002, p.27). Credit has directly and indirectly affected by the education pattern (Jugale, V.B. 1992, p.86). Some studies revealed that the borrowers with lesser education had fear consciousness and had respect to the laws of the land hence they were regular repayers (Prasad, J.V.S. et.al.: 1987, p. 5).

Table 4.4

Education Status of Respondents in Sample Districts

Educational level	*Dindugal*	*Nagapattinam*	*Total*
No formal education	-	3(1.1)	3(0.5)
Primary	17(4.8)	15(5.7)	32(5.2)
Secondary	42(11.9)	11(4.2)	53(8.6)
Higher Secondary	51(14.5)	58(22.1)	109(17.7)
Degree & Professional courses	242(68.8)	175(66.8)	417(67.9)
Total	352(100)	262(100)	614(100)

Source: Data compiled from respondents schedule.

Note: Figures in brackets are percentage to respective total

The role of literacy in boosting NFS was emphasized by Fisher (1997). A well–educated workforce is crucial for the dynamic growth of the NFS (Usha Tuteja: 2004). Proportion of illiterate workers in NFS is much less than that in agriculture (Chadha, 1993, p. 296). To alleviate rural poverty and unemployment, the growth of NFS is desirable which is possible by reducing both dispersion of land and rural assets by land reforms and dispersion in rural income by expansion of primary and secondary education. (Kishore C. Samal: 2000).

Educational status, as an Independent variable enhances the knowledge of an Individual. It also helps the individual to have exposure to mass media develop conduct with change agents, avail benefits under government schemes etc.

It was found that majority of the respondent in both districts have completed either degree or professional courses. This trend reveals that:

(1) NFS have become attractive destination for self employment, and

(2) The entry of competent people would be able to further the growth of NFS in the sample districts.

Family Size

In Indian society, it is the obligation of parents to conduct marriage for their adult children at least after their 21 years of age. In the social context, it is the prelude to the family formation, expansion or even bifurcation. After marriage, there is a transition in the status of men and women with attendant rights and obligations.

The family background plays an important role in moulding the behaviour of its members. The family provides the recognition and security for the individuals as also their identity. The living arrangements are very crucial for the socio-economic status of a person.

There have been a number of studies showing the relationship between the family size and borrowings. The family size of the beneficiaries also related to the repayment performance (Chidambaram, K.: 1999, p. 5). The defaulter group families were found to be of large size and caught in the vicious circle of the mundane realities of life, which might be a reason for their failure to use the loan productivity

(Namasivayam, D. and Ramachandraiah, G.: 2000, p. 419). However, the relationship between the family size and the nature of default has not been found to be quite significant (Joy Joseph Puthuserry: 1999, p.9). Total Number of members in the family influences the income and expenditure pattern of the family.

Table 4.5

Family Size of the Respondents in Sample Districts

Number of members	*Dindugal*	*Nagapattinam*	*Total*
Below 4	134(38.1)	117(44.7)	251(40.9)
Above 4	218(61.9)	145(55.3)	363(59.1)
Total	352(100)	262(100)	614(100)

Source: Data compiled from respondents schedule.

Note: Figures in brackets are percentage to respective total.

It was found that majority of the respondent in both the sample districts belong to the category of above four members in the family. There is no much difference in this case between the districts. Since the respondents selected for this study belong to rural area the factor "every additional member in the family is a additional bread winner for a family", might have influenced the size of the family of the respondent in the sample districts.

Mass Media Exposure

The information revolution has been bringing change in rural life. The village tea-shops remain the common meeting centres for the rural folk. They offer the Dailies, the radio and T.V. services for customers. The State Government has provided T. V. sets to all the panchayats and majority of rural households for public information services. Transport remains unattractive without the T.V., or FM facilities. The exposure to the mass media enabled the people to understand the day-to-day developments regarding the social welfare measures and economic schemes concerning their daily life.

Mass Media play an important role in generating awareness on NFS among the people. Exposure to mass media kindles the interest of the individuals to get exposed to the employment potentialities of NFS.

Table 4.6
Exposure to Mass Media of Respondents in Sample Districts

Frequency	*Dindugal*	*Nagapattinam*	*Total*
Regularly	301(85.5)	45(17.2)	346(56.3)
Occasionally	16(4.5)	93(35.5)	109(17.8)
Rarely	35(10.0)	85(32.4)	120(19.5)
Never	-	39(14.9)	39(6.4)
Grand total	352(100)	262(100)	614(100)

Source: Data compiled from respondents schedule.

Note: Figures in brackets are percentage to respective total.

The study found that majority of the respondent in the sample districts was having exposure its mass media. The level of exposure was high among the respondent in Dindugal District compared to Nagapattinam district. This must be due to the other factors like circulation level of print media, the density of viewers for electronic media and the role of development agents.

Contact with Change Agents

The Government, Non-Government Organizations and Cooperatives are change agents of the village economy. The contact established by an individual with these agents enhances his or her access to various programmes and facilitates his or her grip over a development process. To measure the contact of the individual with the change agents, the following questions were asked: Do the Government Officials come to your village to meet the public? Do the Non-Government Officials come to your village to meet the public? Have you met any of them any time? In a month how many times are you meeting them?

Change agents play an important role in bringing the decided level of change among the people. The Government agencies, Non-governmental Organizations, Educational Institutions, Health Centers, Community Centres, Charity Organizations etc., are considered here as change agents.

Table 4.7

Contact with Change Agents of Respondents in Sample Districts

Opinion	*Dindugal*	*Nagapattinam*	*Total*
Yes	352(100)	71(27)	423(68.8)
No	--	191(73)	191(31.2)
Total	352(100)	262(100)	614(100)

Source : Data compiled from respondents schedule.

Note: Figures in brackets are percentage to respective total.

The study found that the role of the NGO's compared to other organizations listed above, in influencing/ developing contact with the people have been high in both the sample districts. The involvement of NGO's in tsunami rehabilitation in the coastal district of Nagapattinam is a witness. Another factor, the number of NGO's registered in Dindugal district is high compared to other districts. While 100 percent of the respondents have established contact with a agents in Dindugal district, only 27 percent of the respondents in Nagapattinam district have established contact with a change agents. Though, the presences of NGO's are found in Nagapattinam district they have been fully concentrating on tsunami rehabilitations.

Duration of Membership

Membership in the grass-root institutional agencies, viz., Cooperatives and SHGs serves as platforms for the blossoming of inherent leadership ability of an individual. Membership also gives a status in the society and develops a team spirit. Further, having more number of membership of a family in a cooperative society brings additional voting rights arising from new membership, the empowerment of women, increased association between family and the institution etc. Above all the additional membership of the family members increased the borrowing capacity of the family. There has been a close link between duration of membership and the success of cooperative societies. For more number of years their association with the business of the cooperative society would be high and they will become loyal to their organization.

Table 4.8
Duration of Membership of Respondents in Sample Districts

Duration of Membership	*Dindugal*	*Nagapattinam*	*Total*
Up to 3 years	14(4.0)	8(3.1)	22(3.5)
4-6 years	35(10.0)	12(4.6)	47(7.6)
7-9 years	101(28.7)	45(17.2)	146(24.0)
Above 10 years	202(57.3)	197(75.1)	399(64.9)
Total	352(100)	262(100)	614(100)

Source: Data compiled from respondents schedule.

Note: Figures in brackets are percentage to respective total.

It is found that majority of the members in both the districts, 57.3 percent in Dindugal and 75.1 percent in Nagapattinam had membership duration of more than one year. Both the districts put together this category was almost 65 percent. Only 3.5 percent of sample members had upto three years of membership. The remaining 31 percent of sample members had upto 4 to 9 years duration of membership.

Borrowing from Institutional Agencies

It was observed that the PCARDBs remained as the mainstay of NFS financing in the study areas. Despite several built-in organizational constraints, the Cooperative Banks still enjoy a unique position in the rural credit market due to their close association with the people and larger clientele base at the grassroots level (Mohan, N.: 2004, p. 390). Contrary to this, few studies revealed that a larger number of loans were obtained from the CBs among the institutional sources whereas only 13 percent of the borrowers had taken from the PACS (Singh, A.K. et.al., 1993, p. 396). The landless artisans and women population remained completely neglected from the Cooperative Movement (Jugale, V.B.: 1994, p. 61). There is no significant difference in the performance of various financial agencies in Madurai District in lending to the agricultural and service sectors such as branches of SBI and its associates, Nationalized and Private Sector Banks and other agencies such as TIIC, Madurai District Central Cooperative Bank Ltd. etc. (Rengaswamy, V. & Ramnath, R.L.: 2000, p. 82).

Both the institution and Non-institution agencies have established net work to provide short term, medium term, and long term of the Rural population. Among the institutional agencies namely, PACB, PCARDB and Commercial Bank, PCARDBs enjoy lion's share in the market for long term credit.

Table 4.9

Borrowings from Institutional Agencies in Sample Districts

Borrowings	*Dindugal*	*Nagapattinam*	*Total*
PACB	215(34.7)	119(30.0)	334(33.0)
PCARDB	352(56.8)	262(66.2)	614(60.4)
CB	21(3.4)	15(3.8)	36(3.5)
SHG	32(5.1)	-	32(3.1)
Total	620(100)	396(100)	1016(100)

Source: Data compiled from respondents schedule.

Note: Figures in brackets are percentage to respective total.

The present study found that sample respondent have availed credit from PACB, PCARDB, CB, SHGs. From this trend it is inferred that

(1) The access to institution credit to the rural borrowers has been increased.

(2) Self Help Groups have been emerging parallel with a salient features both institutional and non-institutional credit.

(3) The increase in the source of credit may in some time increase the debt burden of the individual than increasing the income.

Functional Analysis

To explain the relationship between the demographic, social and economic variables and employment and income generation, the functional analysis was carried out.

Employment Generation Function

Employment generated through NFS is taken as the dependent variable. In order to construct a function to express the variations on employment generation, the simple correlation analysis was carried out with each one of the ten variables viz., sex, age, education, family size, mass media exposure, contact with change agents, duration of membership, borrowings, investments and the interaction variable borrowing X investment with employment generation. The correlation analysis confirmed the inclusion of the above set of variables with the employment generation on a linear regression for Dindugal and Nagapattinam Districts.

The mathematical form of the estimated employment generation equation for Dindugal District is:

$$Y_1 = 1.257 + 0.025^{NS} X_1 + 0.183^{*} X_2 + 0.042 X_3 - 0.036^{NS} X_4 + 0.216^{*} X_5 + 0.063^{*} X_6 + 0.085^{*} X_7 + 0.314^{**} X_8 + 0.229^{**} X_9 + 0.881^{**} X_{10},$$

R-Square = 0.513**

N = 352

The statistical details pertaining to the above functions are presented below in table 4.10.

Table 4.10

Employment Generation in Dindugal District

Sl. No.	*Name of the variable*	*Symbol used*	*'b' values*	*Standard error*	*'t'*	*Level of significance*
1	Sex	X_1	0.025	0.027	0.916	NS
2	Age	X_2	0.183	0.095	1.923	*
3	Education	X_3	0.042	0.021	2.014	*
4	Family Size	X_4	- 0.036	+0.032	- 1.113	NS
5	Mass media exposure	X_5	0.216	0.101	2.147	*
6	Contact with change agents	X_6	0.063	0.031	2.001	*
7	Duration of Membership	X_7	0.085	0.043	1.992	*
8	Borrowings	X_8	0.314	0.099	3.146	**
9	Investments	X_9	0.229	0.070	3.271	**
10	Borrowings X Investments	X_{10}	0.881	0.098	3.873	**
11	Regression constant	b_o	1.257	-	-	-

R-Square = 0.513** N = 352

The R square is 0.513 which is significant at 1 per cent level of probability. This implies that 51.3 per cent of the variations in the employment generation is being explained by the ten independent variables considered in the study. The regression coefficient is significant for the variables age, education, mass media exposure, contact with change agents, duration of membership, borrowings, investments and the interaction term. The positive significant coefficient for the age, at 5 per cent level of probability implies that increase in the age helps in generating employment in the NFS in which the investments are made. The regression coefficient for education is also significant at 5 per cent level of probability. This implies that a unit increase in the educational level of the respondent cetaris parbus could bring an increase of 0.042 units in the employment generation i.e., approximately 1.3 hours.

The regression coefficient for the variable mass media exposure is also positive and significant at 5 per cent level of probability. This implies that additional exposure to mass media helps in generation of additional man days.

The regression coefficient for the variable contact with change agents is positive and significant at 5 per cent level of probability, which implies that an additional contact with the Change Agents cetaris parbus could bring 0.063 units (approximately ½ hour) of additional man days of employment generation.

The regression coefficient for duration of membership is also positive and significant at 5 per cent level of probability. This implies that one year increase in the duration of membership cetaris parbus could bring an increase of 0.085 (0.68 hours) units of man days of employment generated.

The regression coefficient for the variable borrowings is positive and significant at 1 per cent level of probability. This implies that a unit increase in the borrowings cetaris parbus could increase the employment generated by 0.314 units (2.5 hours) of man days.

The regression coefficient for the variable Investments is also positive and significant at 1 per cent level of probability. This implies that a unit increase in the investments cetaris paribus would result an increase of 0.229 units (approximately 1.8 hours) of man days in the employment.

The interaction term coefficient is also positive and significant at 1 per cent level of probability. This implies that when borrowing invested properly would result in highest employment generation, through NFS.

Similar analysis with the same set of variables carried out for the Nagapattinam District resulted in the following.

The mathematical form of the estimated employment generation equation for Nagapattinam District is:

$$Y_1 = 0.843 + 0.032^{NS} X_1 + 0.094^{*} X_2 + 0.039^{*} X_3 - 0.042^{NS} X_4 + 0.119^{NS} X_5 + 0.032^{NS} X_6 + 0.041^{*} X_7 + 0.142^{**} X_8 + 0.112^{**} X_9 + 0.192^{**} X_{10},$$

R-Square = 0.463^{**}

N = 262

The statistical details pertaining to the above, functions are presented below in Table 4.11.

Table 4.11

Employment Generation in Nagapattinam District

Sl. No.	*Name of the variable*	*Symbol used*	*'b' values*	*Standard error*	*'t'*	*Level of significance*
1	Sex	X_1	0.032	0.049	0.652	NS
2	Age	X_2	0.094	0.049	1.909	*
3	Education	X_3	0.039	0.018	2.116	*
4	Family Size	X_4	-0.042	-0.0.38	1.085	NS
5	Mass media exposure	X_5	0.119	0.119	0.993	NS
6	Contact with change agents	X_6	0.032	0.052	0.615	NS
7	Duration of Membership	X_7	0.041	0.018	2.163	*
8	Borrowings	X_8	0.142	0.062	2.264	*
9	Investments	X_9	0.112	0.052	2.147	*
10	Borrowings X Investments	X_{10}	0.192	0.086	2.225	*
11	Regression constant	b_o	0.843	-	-	-

R-Square = 0.463* N = 262

Here R Square is 0.463 which is significant at 1 per cent level of probability. This implies that the set of independent variables selected could explain 46.3 per cent of the variations in the employment generations. In this case the regression coefficient is significant for age, education, duration of membership, borrowings, investments and borrowings and investments. The magnitude of the coefficient makes us to infer that as the age increases it has positive effect on the employment generation. Similarly education has also positive effect. That is a unit increase in the level of education cetaris paribus would result in an increase of 0.018 units (0.14 hours) of employment generation. The regression coefficient for the variable duration of membership is also positive and significant at 5 per cent level of probability. This implies that an additional one year of the duration of membership cetaris paribus would result in 0.018 units (0.14 hours) of employment generation.

The regression coefficient for the variable borrowings is positive and significant at 5 per cent level of probability. This implies that a unit increase in the borrowings cetaris parbus could increase the employment generated by 0.062 units (1/2 hours of man days).

The regression coefficient for the variable Investments is also positive and significant at 5 per cent level of probability. This implies that a unit increase in the investments cetaris paribus would result in an increase of 0.052 units (approximately 0.41 hours of man days) in the employment.

The interaction term coefficient is also positive and significant at 5 per cent level of probability. This implies that when borrowing invested properly would result in highest employment generation.

Comparing the results obtained in Dindugal and Nagapattinam Districts it is inferred that in Dindugal District except the variable sex and the family size all others had positive contribution towards employment generation in NFS. In the case of Nagapattinam District apart from the above said two variables for Dindugal District, additionally mass media and contact with change agents also do not have significant coefficient.

The magnitude of the corresponding regression coefficients and the level of significance are lesser in Nagapattinam District.

Age is positive and significant in both the districts. Here, additional age, is an implication of maturity and experience which makes him to have better contacts which in turn might help in investments with better returns. Same is the case with education i.e., additional educational qualification will help them to go and approach people and get the needed information to increase the returns to scale.

Similarly duration of membership is also a proxy for experience.

Income Generation Function

The mathematical form of the estimated income generation equation for Dindugal District is:

$$Y_2 = 2.426 + 0.013^{**} X_1 + 0.117^{*} X_2 + 0.026^{*} X_3 + 0.012^{NS} X_4 + 0.192^{*} X_5 + 0.046^{*} X_6 + 0.052^{*} X_7 + 0.083^{*} X_8 + 0.056^{*} X_9 + 0.118^{**} X_{10}$$

R-Square = 0.461**

N = 352

The statistical details pertaining to the above functions are presented below in table 4.12.

Table 4.12

Income Generation in Dindugal District

Sl. No.	*Name of the variable*	*Symbol used*	*'b' values*	*Standard error*	*'t'*	*Level of significance*
1	Sex	X_1	0.013	0.006	2.082	*
2	Age	X_2	0.117	0.061	1.916	*
3	Education	X_3	0.026	0.012	2.117	*
4	Family Size	X_4	0.012	0.13	0.946	NS
5	Mass media exposure	X_5	0.192	0.86	2.227	*
6	Contact with change agents	X_6	0.046	0.024	1.946	*
7	Duration of Membership	X_7	0.052	0.024	2.164	*
8	Borrowings	X_8	0.083	0.037	2.218	*
9	Investments	X_9	0.056	0.025	2.226	*
10	Borrowings X Investments	X_{10}	0.118	0.041	2.372	**
11	Regression constant	b_o	2.426	-	-	-

R-Square = 0.461** N = 352

The details presented above, revealed that R Square is 0.461, which is significant at 1 per cent level of probability. This implies that 46.1 per cent of the variations in the income generation is being explained by the ten independent variables included in the function. Except family size, the regression coefficient is positive and significant for all the other variables.

The regression coefficient for the variable number of units invested indicates that as the number of investments gets increased the income also gets increased. Here an additional unit brings 0.013 unit of additional income. The coefficient for the variable age indicates that additional age helps in additional income generation.

The regression coefficient for the variable education also indicates that the education has a positive effect on income generation. As in the earlier cases the family size has no contribution for income generation also.

Mass media exposure, contact with change agents, duration of membership, borrowings, investments, and the interaction have positive effects on the income generation.

The mathematical form of the estimated income generation equation for Nagapattinam District is:

$$Y_2 = 1.987 + 0.026^* X_1 + 0.082^* X_2 + 0.024^* X_3 + 0.002^{NS} X_4 + 0.008^{NS} X_5 + 0.028^{NS} X_6 + 0.046^* X_7 + 0.061^* X_8 + 0.037^* X_9 + 0.101^* X_{10}$$

R-Square = 0.396**

N = 262

The statistical details pertaining to the above, functions are presented below in table 4.13.

Table 4.13

Income Generation in Nagapattinam District

Sl. No.	*Name of the variable*	*Symbol used*	*'b' values*	*Standard error*	*'t'*	*Level of significance*
1	Sex	X_1	0.026	0.012	2.165	*
2	Age	X_2	0.082	0.036	2.243	*
3	Education	X_3	0.024	0.011	2.051	*
4	Family Size	X_4	0.002	0.002	1.116	NS

5	Mass media exposure	X_5	0.008	0.051	0.195	NS
6	Contact with change agents	X_6	0.028	0.031	0.893	NS
7	Duration of Membership	X_7	0.046	0.021	2.165	*
8	Borrowings	X_8	0.061	0.028	2.142	*
9	Investments	X_9	0.037	0.016	2.228	*
10	Borrowings X Investments	X_{10}	0.101	0.043	2.349	*
11	Regression constant	b_0	1.987	-	-	-

R-Square = 0.396** N = 262

In the case of Nagapattinam District, the R.Square for the fitted equation is 0.396 which is significant at 1 per cent level of probability. This implies that 39.6 per cent of the variations in the income generation is being explained by the ten independent variables included in the function. Except the variables family size and contact with change agents and mass media all others have positive and significant coefficients indicating their positive effects on the income generation.

Comparing the results in the two districts there is identical behaviour except in the case of contact with the change agents in Nagapattinam which makes no impact in this district.

Performance Analysis

Employment Generation Performance

The results obtained from the analysis are ranked based on the performance of the variables and presented in table 4.5. As far as the employment generation is concerned in the order of performance in the two districts are almost identical. In both the districts investment through borrowings has the highest bearing on employment generation. Next in the order comes borrowing for the both the districts. Similarly investment is derived as the third in both the districts. In the case of the Dindugal mass media has an impact which is not so in Nagapattinam. This might be due to the higher level of literacy existing in the study area in the Dindugal district. Thus as far as the performance analysis is concerned there is no variation between districts in the order of performance. However, the rate is higher in Dindugal than in Nagapattinam, this might be due to the constant efforts taken by PCARDBs in Dindugal in the proper utilization of loan amounts as well as the number of PCARDBs functioning in the district.

Income Generation Performance

In the case of the income generation, in both the districts the investment through borrowings has occupied the first position. In Dindugal the borrowings occupied the second place whereas the borrowing is in the third place in Nagapattinam District. For Nagapattinam District the second important factor is age, which has no dominant role in Dindugal District. Mass media has a third place in Dindugal, whereas it has no role in Nagapattinam. Similarly investment is in the fourth place in Dindugal whereas it has no role in Nagapattinam District. In Napattinam the duration of membership occupies fourth place. The entry of age and duration of membership in the Nagapattinam District might be that the higher duration of membership and higher age might have helped these people to get information on proper investment NFS. The effect of age in Nagapattinam District might be that there is higher level of labour migration among the younger in this coastal district.

Poverty Assessment

In order to know as how poverty can be eradicated through NFS activities, it was decided to find the direct and indirect effects of each one of the variables which are highly related to income generated through NFS. Of all the variables selected the coefficient of correlation was highest for education of the respondents, exposure to mass media, contact with change agents and the average education level of other family adults.

The path analysis was carried out with the above four variables. The direct effects and substantial indirect effects are presented below in table 4.14. In the case of Dindugal District, the result is:

Table 4.14

Results of Path Analysis in Dindugal District

Sl. No.	*Name of the variable*	*Symbols used*	*Direct Path*	*Substantial Indirect effects* I	II	III
1	Educational level of the respondents	X_1	0.312	0.053 X_2	0.021 X_3	0.009 X_4
2	Exposure to Mass Media	X_2	0.287'	0.048 X_3	0.019 X_1	0.007 X_1
3	Contact with Change Agents	X_3	0.243	0.051 X_2	0.022 X_1	0.005 X_2
4	Average educational level of adults in the family	X_4	0.112	0.037 X_1	0.011 X_2	0.004 X_3

All the included variables have positive direct effects and indirect effects. In the order the direct effect is highest for education, second comes exposure to mass media, while contact with change agents is in the third and average educational level of adults in the family is the last. In the case of indirect effects the maximum level is in the first column in which the mass media exposure has occurred twice. This implies that any variable if interacted with mass media exposure could help in the reduction of poverty. Similar explanations can be given for the other two indirect effects. That is reading in column 2 indicates that the level of education of the respondents is another factor which helps indirectly also. Thus the study revealed that education combined with exposure to mass media would result in poverty reduction.

The following table explains the position for Nagapattinam District.

Table 4.15

Results of Path Analysis in Nagapattinam District

Sl. No.	*Name of the variable*	*Symbols used*	*Direct Path*	*Substantial Indirect effects I*	*II*	*III*
1	Educational level of the respondents	X_1	0.256	0.056 X_3	0.032 X_3	0.008 X_2
2	Exposure to Mass Media	X_2	0.300	0.041 X_3	0.026 X_1	0.011 X_4
3	Contact with Change Agents	X_3	0.352	0.021 X_2	0.018 X_2	0.008 X_4
4	Average educational level of adults in the family	X_4	0.221	0.033 X_2	0.031 X_1	0.014 X_3

All the included variables have positive direct effects and indirect effects. In the order the direct effect is highest for contact with change agents followed by exposure to mass media, third comes the level of education of the respondents and the last is the average educational level of the adults in the family. Among the indirect effects the maximum contribution is by exposure to mass media and contact with change agents. Thus in the case of Nagapattinam district for alleviating poverty, change agents should also concentrate on giving exposure to mass media.

Change in Income Position of the respondents: Before and After

In order to test whether the borrowing and investment on NFS helped the respondents to improve their economic status, the mean and standard deviation of their income before availing the loan and after utilizing the loan are estimated and presented for the two districts, viz., Dindugal and Nagapattinam in Table 4.16 and Table 4.17, respectively, below:

Table 4.16

Details of Income for Dindugal District

Parameter	*Before Availing the loan*	*After utilizing the loan*
Mean	12501.23	21232.13
Standard Deviation	2816.42	3419.72

N= 352

Table 4.17

Details of Income for Nagapattinam District

Parameter	*Before Availing the loan*	*After utilizing the loan*
Mean	11201.11	19418.37
Standard Deviation	2401.90	3219.92

N= 262

To know whether loan availed for NFS has helped the sample respondents in improving their economic status the simple 't' test was applied for both the tables. The estimated 't' values are:

't' = 36.97 for Dindugal District and
't' = 33.11 for Nagapattinam District

In both the cases the 't' value is significant at 1 per cent level of probability. This shows that the impact of loan utilized on NFS improved the economic status of the sample respondents. This proved the hypothesis that NFS helped in income generation in rural areas.

Availability of Employment to the Respondents (Before and After)

In order to test whether the borrowing and investment on NFS helped the respondents to get regular employment, the mean and standard deviation of their availability of employment before availing the loan and after utilizing the loan are estimated and presented for the two districts, viz., Dindugal and Nagapattinam in Table 4.18 and Table 4.19, respectively, below,

Table 4.18

Details of Employment for Dindugal District

Parameter	*Before Availing the loan*	*After utilizing the loan*
Mean	96.3	163.2
Standard Deviation	12.5	16.7

N= 352

Table 4.19

Details of Employment for Nagapattinam District

Parameter	*Before Availing the loan*	*After utilizing the loan*
Mean	82.5	146.8
Standard Deviation	11.3	14.8

N= 262

To know whether the loan availed for NFS has helped the sample respondents by providing employment for more number of days, the't' test was applied here also for both the tables. The estimated't' values are:

't' = 60.21 for Dindugal District and

't' = 52.96 for Nagapattinam District

In both the cases the't' value are significant at 1 per cent level of probability. This shows that the loan utilized on NFS increased employment (number of mandays) to the sample respondents. This proved the hypothesis that NFS helped in employment generation in rural areas.

Conclusion

There is correlation between socio-economic profile of individuals and access to institutional credit and employment generation through NFS. From the above analysis it is found that age, education, duration of membership, borrowings and investments had positively contributed towards employment generation through NFS among the sample respondents in Dindugal and Nagapattinam Districts. It is also found that NFS loans provided by sample PCARDBs in these districts have helped the sample respondents to generate employment and income. Hence, it is concluded that NFS could exist and spread breaking geographical barriers for generating employment and income among the people in which the role of PCARDBs would be significant.

5

Findings, Conclusion and Suggestions

This chapter presents the major findings of the study and conclusion arrived at. Based on these certain suggestions are made to promote NFS through PCARDBs.

Findings

The salient findings of the study are presented hereunder.

1. It was found that at all India level the structure of long term credit is not uniform. Federal, unitary, mixed and integrated structure exists at present. As such there were 663 branches of SCARDBs functioning in our country during the year 2000–02. This has increased to 887 branches in 2001–02 and came down to 791 in 2004–05.
2. In the case of owned funds, it was found that in the year 2000–01, the total owned fund of SCARDBs at All India level was Rs. 2386 crores. This had increased over the years and stood at Rs. 3549 crores in 2004–05.
3. It was found that these ARDBs are not concentrating on deposit mobilization which is evident from the fact that the total deposits mobilized was Rs. 535

crores in 2000–01. This has grown over the years and stood at Rs. 608 crores in 2004–05.

4. Due to Government waiving policies across the country, the total loan issued by the structure was affected severely.
5. It was found that the total number of PCARDBS functioning in the country as on 2000–01 was 732. This had increased to 768 in 2004–05. The total owned funds of the PCARDBs also increased from Rs. 867 crores to Rs.1782 crores during the study period. However there was marked increase in borrowings during the study period, i.e. from Rs. 8396 crores to Rs.12933 crores. The loan outstanding was on the increasing trend indicating the poor recovery of loans. This is evident from the fact that the position of NPA both at SCARDB and PCARDB level have been at an increasing trend.
6. The total NPA at SCARDBs level was Rs. 2850.56 crores in 2000–01, which has increased to Rs. 5437.38 crores in 2004–05. The respective figures for PCARDBs were Rs. 2004.77 crores and Rs. 4055.91 crores.
7. The increasing trend is NPA have worsened the financial visibility of ARDBs, because a huge reserve in the form of provisioning is made due to NPAs.
8. In the case of Tamilnadu the LT structure consisted of Tamilandu State Agriculture and Rural Development Bank (TNSCRD) and 181 PCARDBs. It was found that the increasing trend in NPA had severely hit the growth of the TNSCARDB. The total NPA as on 2001–02 was Rs. 505.85 crores, which had grown over the years and stood at Rs. 892.75 crores as on 2005 – 06, i.e., 88.26 percent to total loan, was outstanding.
9. The cumulative loss of TNSCARDBs was also on the increasing trend for the study period, which was Rs. 45.25 crores in the year 2001–02 and gone to the extent of Rs. 155.69 crores in the year 2005–06.

10. A general recession in the loan operations of PCARDBs was found during the study period. This was due to Government waiving policies and consequent impact on recovery and recycling of funds. For example the total loan issued during the year 2000–01 was Rs. 20093.43 lakhs, which was 0.60 per cent less than the previous year. The total loan issued during the year 2004–05 was Rs. 1243.96 lakhs, which was 90.20 percent less than the previous year. From the above analysis, it was found that the functions of ARDBs structure at all levels were severely affected. The reason for this morbid growth were, (a) loan waiving policies of the Governments (b) entry of new generation banks in rural finance and (c) politicization and bureaucratizes of cooperative movement.
11. While analyzing the performance of sample PCARDBs with regard to coverage of membership it was found that Mayiladuthurai PCARDB faired better while comparing their counterparts in Nagapattinam district. In the case of Dindugal district, Dindugal PCARDB faired better than others. As the growth of membership is directly linked with the loan operations, the growth in membership pictured the growth of the banks.
12. The trend in the position of paid up share capital of PCARDB in Nagapattinam district showed that Mayiladuthurai PCARDB faired better than their counterparts by mobilizing paid up share capital to the tune of Rs. 50.63 lakhs as on 2005–06. The trend in the position of paid up share capital of the PCARDBs in Dindugal showed that Palani PCARDBs could be able to mobilize share capital more than the district average, during the study period. Though Reddiyarchatram PCARDB maintained high proportion of borrowing members compared to others they could not mobilize shares like others throughout the study period.

13. While analyzing the performance of PCARDBs in the creation of reserve fund, it was found that Sirkali PCARDB created more reserve fund than others in Nagapattinam district. Whereas in Dindugal district compared to the reserve position in other PCARDB, the reserve position in Dindugal PCARDB was better.
14. It was found that the average borrowing per bank at district level was Rs.303.03 lakhs in Dindugal district in 2005-06. Palani PCARDBs was found to have borrowed more than district average during the study period. Also, it was found that there was high correlation between borrowings and loan issued at the district level. It showed that the PCARDBs depended upon only borrowing from SCARDB as a major source for lending.
15. The position of borrowings in PCARDBs in Ngapattinam district showed decreasing trend over the years. The condition was worse in the case of Sirkali PCARDB. This trend had negative effect on the loan portfolio.
16. The trend in the working capital in PCARDBs in Dindugal district showed that the Vedasandur PCARDB followed by Palani PCARDB had higher level of working capital than the district average i.e., Rs. 497.75 lakhs.
17. The trend in the working capital position of PCARDBs in Nagapattinam district showed that the position of working capital in Mayiladuthurai PCARDB was better than its counterparts in the district.
18. As a Government policy the elected board of management of PCARDBs was superseded and Government officials are appointed as Special Officers to manage the affairs of the sample banks. The special officers were assisted by a team of paid employees of concerned PACRDBs. At present only three cadre of paid employees are in service viz., Secretary, Supervisors and Office Assistants. This structure has

also been rationalized and at present the service of Office Assistants is out-sourced.

19. The performance in loan operation of sample PCARDBs showed morbid growth. It was found that Sirkali PCARDB in Nagapattinam and Palani PCARDBs in Dindugal district had provided loan more than their respective counterparts. Further, it is to be noted here that from the year 2004–05 Kodaikanal PCARDB from 2005–06 all PCARDBs in Dindugal district had not provided any loans due to poor recovery climate.

20. It was found that the position of overdue in sample PCARDBs in Dindugal and Nagapattinam district was serious.

21. It was found that SCARDB hold major share in NABARD refinance for RNFS during the year 2001-02 whereas, CBs dominated in the scene during 2005-06 at all India level. In the case of Tamilnadu the State Cooperative Bank availed more refinance under this scheme from NABARD. As the NABARD's refinance was linked with recovery level, the poor recovery at ARDBs level affected their eligibility for refinance. Hence the share of SCARDBs had come down over the years.

22. The Region wise analysis showed that the Southern Region which consists of Andrapredesh, Karnataka, Kerala, Pandichery, Lakshadweep and Tamilnadu availed more refinance compared to other regions in India upto the year 2004–05 for RNFS. The Northern Region which consists of Chandigarh, New Delhi, Haryana, Himachal Pradesh, Jammu and Kashmir, Punjab and Rajasthan availed more refinance under NFS during the year 2005-06 followed by the east region. This trend revealed that NFS as a breeder of employment opportunity had attracted the attention of people across the country.

23. It was found that at national level the major NFS sectors, which attracted refinance during the past from NABARD were:
    1) Traditional Industries
    2) Agro Processing/Agro Industries
    3) Handicrafts
    4) Handlooms
    5) Engineering Industries
    6) Building/Construction Materials
    7) Modern Activities
    8) Transport Vehicles
    9) Service Activities
    10) Rural Housing
    11) Other Miscellaneous sectors.

    Among these industries major segment of the refinance went to transport vehicles upto year 2000-01. From 2001-02 to 2005-06, rural housing projects dominated the scene.
24. In the case of long term credit structure the lending for NFS was started in Tamilnadu by SCARDB from the year 1991. The available figure showed that NFS had not received much attention.
25. At the State level it was found that the total agricultural loans issued by PCARDBs in Tamilnadu increased from Rs. 20093.43 crores to Rs. 21791.62 crores during the period 2000-01 to 2002-03. The total NFS loans issued by PCARDBs increased from Rs.5573.26 crores to 5909.37 crores during the same period. There after the total agricultural loan as well as NFS loan issued had come down heavily and the percentage of NFS loans in the total loans had come down to 9.28 from 27 per cent during the year 2000-01.
26. It is found that NFS had not received due recognition. The constraints for the slow growth of NFS in this

State were;

- ❖ Frequent interruption in power supply
- ❖ Inadequate number of common work sheds
- ❖ Inadequate marketing infrastructure/support, especially for handicrafts products
- ❖ Inadequate mapping of resource based potential areas for NFS development
- ❖ Pollution caused by concentration of power loom units and delay of commissioning of common effluent treatment plans
- ❖ Lack of effective coordination among promotional, regulatory and financial institutions Inadequate/absence of timely credit flow to the sector, leading to cost over runs.

27. It was found that all categories of loans were issued by PCARDBs in Dindugal district under NFS, namely Composite Loans, Integrated Loans, Small Road Transport Operations (SRTO) Loans and Other Loans. Invariably all the sample banks had issued more loans for SRTO, because of clear title, easy procedure, bankable return on investment comparatively higher than other NFS activities, assured repayment, attachment of asset was easy in case of default, and above all increasing demand among members.

28. It was found that NFS operations would reduce the overdue risk and help the institution to continue their business. But in reality NFS loan operation too were not away from the problem of overdue.

29. It was found from the study that in Nagapattinam district 52.8 percent of the NFS loan demand was overdue in 2001 – 02, which has increased to 64 percent in 2005 – 06. The individual bank wise analysis showed that the problem was serious in Sirkali PCARDB, where, more than 96 percent of the NFS loan demand was overdue.

30. In the case of Dindugal district almost all NFS loans

had become overdue. For example in all PCARDBs the percentage of FNS loan overdue to loan demand was about more than ninety percent. This proved that NFS loans too are vulnerable to the problem of overdue.

31. It was found that both the members and employees perceived certain problems in NFS. Members perceived that defective asset valuation norms and procedure, time consuming procedures, high cost of borrowings, delay in loan sanction, loans not available as and when required were the major problem. Employees perception on NFS loan operations were, identification of potential entrepreneurs, competition in rural credit financial market, target approach in lending, absence of democratic governance and command of pressure groups.

32. It was found that the problems associated with designing the NFS lending seemed to have caused by factors which were beyond the purview of PCARDBs. They warranted policy interventions.

33. The study found that 87 per cent of the respondent of the study were male. The district wise analysis showed no much difference. The number of women respondent represented in the sample was very poor.

34. It was found that in Dindugal district majority of the respondents belonged to the category of more than 50 years of age. Contradictory to this trend, majority of the respondents in Nagapattinam District belonged to the age group of 36-50. In both the districts the participation of the younger generation i.e., the respondents belonged to the age group of less than 35, was poor.

35. The study found that majority of the respondent in both the regions belonged to MBC and BC. Only 8.3 per cent of the sample respondents belonged to weaker sections. It was found that labour migration was the major reason among these communities for not availing loans for NFS activities.

36. It was found that majority of the respondents in both districts had completed either degree or professional courses. This trend revealed that: (a) NFS had become attractive destination for self employment and (b) The entry of competent people would be able to further the growth of NFS in the sample districts.
37. It was found that majority of the respondents in both the sample districts belonged to the category of above four members in the family. There was not much difference in this case between the sample districts. Since the respondents selected for this study belonged to rural area the factor "every additional member in the family is a additional bread winner for a family", might have influenced the size of the family of the respondent in the sample districts.
38. The study found that majority of the respondent in the sample districts was having exposure to mass media. The level of exposure was high among the respondent in Dindugal District compared to Nagapattinam district. This might be due to other factors like circulation level of print media, the density of viewers for electronic media, and the role of development agents.
39. The study found that the role of the NGO's compared to other organizations in influencing / developing contact with the people had been high in both the sample districts. Another factor, the number of NGO's registered in Dindugal district was high compared to other districts. While 100 percent of the respondents had established contact with change agents in Dindugal district, only 27 per cent of the respondents in Nagapattinam district had established contact with change agents. Though, the presents of NGO's were found in Nagapattinam district they were fully concentrating on tsunami rehabilitations.
40. There was a close link between duration of membership and the success of cooperative societies.

For more number of years their association with the business of the cooperative society would be high and they would become loyal to their organization.

41. The present study found that sample respondent had availed credit from PACB, PCARDB, CB and SHGs. From this trend it is inferred that (a) the access to institutional credit to the rural borrowers have been increased (b) Self Help Groups have been emerging parallel in rural credit market with a salient features of both institutional and non-institutional credit and (c) the increase in the source of credit may some time increase the debt burden of the individual than increasing the income.
42. In Dindugal District except the variable sex and the family size all others had positive contribution towards employment generation in NFS. In the case of Nagapattinam District apart from the above said two variables for Dindugal District, additionally mass media and contact with change agents did not have significant coefficients.
43. It was found that in the case of performance analysis there was no variation between districts in the order of performance. However, the rate was higher in Dindugal than Nagapattinam, which might be due to the constant efforts taken by PCARDBs in Dindugal in the proper utilization of loan amounts as well as the number of PCARDBs run. This implied that any variable if interacted with mass media exposure could help in the reduction of poverty. Thus the study revealed that education combined with exposure to mass media would result in poverty reduction.
44. In the case of Nagapattinam district for alleviating poverty, change agents should also concentrate in giving exposure to mass media.
45. It was found that the impact of loan utilized on NFS improved the economic status of the sample

respondents. This proved the hypothesis that NFS helped in income generation in rural areas.

46. It was found that the loan utilized on NFS increased employment (number of man days) to the sample respondents. This proved the hypothesis that NFS helped in employment generation in rural areas.

Conclusion

The present study found that the socio, economic and infrastructural facilities available in the sample districts are bankable. It means there is greater scope for any financial institutions to expand its market. The role of cooperatives in general and PCARDBs in particular in the socioeconomic development of the State need not be over emphasized. In fact in India, the first PACS was registered in Thirur village of Tamilnadu soon after the enactment of Cooperative Credit Societies Act in 1904. In this context, all the PCARDBs in sample district were registered during colonial era itself. With the long years of experience in rural finance the sample PCARDBs have contributed to the socio economic development of the sample districts by providing needed long term finance. This was found during Focus Group Discussions held with the sample respondents. However, the anti-cooperative policies of the successive State Governments (not allowing cooperatives to function fully and freely as per ICA Principles), and its impact on the perceptions of general public on the functions of ARDBs have affected the functions of ARDBs. These trends have affected the business of sample PCARDBs as well. But, the emergence of NFS, as absorber of excessive workforce in rural areas, provides scope for expansion of business of PCARDBs. PCARDBs have identified NFS as a viable area for diversification. But they have yet to harvest the opportunities both at State and at Primary level. The NFS loan operations at PCARDBs level showed that NFS loan was meant only for SRTO, neglecting the potential of other areas. It is time that the potentiality of NFS must be realized and harvested early by PCARDBs otherwise new players will enter into NFS market. At the same time it is to be noted that NFS loan has generated employment and income among the sample respondents in both the districts. However, the present approach in NFS lending need to be redesigned in a user-friendly manner.

Suggestions

The present study offers following suggestions to promote NFS through PCARDBs.

1. Backward and Forward Linkages

The PCARDBs system can draw strength and support to tune the NFS loan operations from various institutions/ bodies, which have dent on rural economy. Since the Panchayati bodies assumed the responsibility of full fledged institutions of self governance at micro level, the ways and means of promotional as well as developmental interactions between PARDBs and PRI may be sculled out. Similarly institutions that are serving as support system for NFS may be identified and suitable policies may be framed at the macro level to maximize the benefits of systems approach

Chart 5 – 1

Loan delivery system for NFS

(A Member-centered Approach)

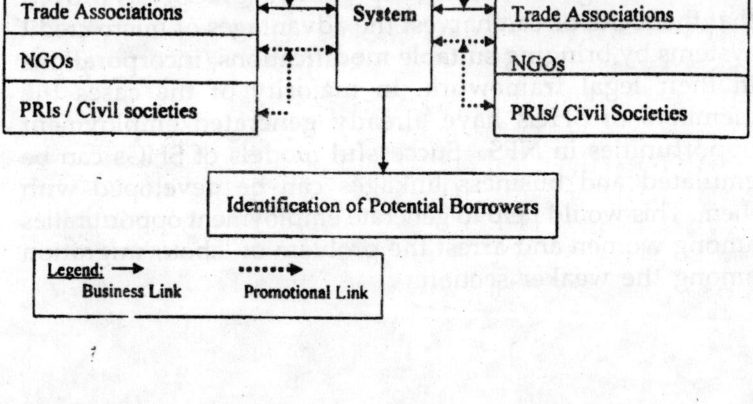

for sustainable development. For this purpose the model suggested in this study may be adopted (Chart 5.1)

2. *Borrower-friendly loaning policies and procedures*

Both the members and employees view that the loaning procedures of PCARDBs in general loans and NFS in particular is 'cumbersome'. The existing procedure aggravates the cost of borrowings besides causing physical strain to borrowers. Hence, borrower-friendly procedures need to be adopted.

3. *Eradication of Non Performing Asset*

The mounting of NPA at PCARDB level and SCARDB level meets great concern. The policy of waiving of loan by successive Government for their political end must be stopped by enacting a suitable law at appropriate level. An in depth study of waiving policies revealed the fact that it has helped big farmers mostly (where their number is small but the amount of loan is greater) rather than small farmers or marginal farmers. Also, the waiving of loans affected adversely the NFS activities by PCARDBs getting funds from their Apex Banks. Stringent action must be taken on the erring members who failed to repay their loans so as to create moral fear in the mind of others, which may reduce the NPAs and in turn it may create a atmosphere for PCARDBs to improve their activities and lend excessively for NFS activities.

4. *Business linkage with SHGs*

The emergence of Self Help Groups (SHGs) has proved that the PARDBs can harvest the advantages of micro credit systems by bringing suitable modifications/incorporations in their legal framework. In majority of the cases the members of SHGs have already generated employment opportunities in NFS. Successful models of SHGs can be emulated and business linkages can be developed with them. This would help to generate employment opportunities among women and arrest the problem of labour migration among the weaker section.

Appendices

Notes

1) The Primary Agricultural Cooperative Credit Societies (PACS) are called as Primary Agricultural Cooperative Banks (PACBs) in Tamil Nadu with effect from Government Notification – G.O. Ms.No.507, COOPERATION (CCI) DEPARTMENT dated: 1.9.1987 and Letter No.32651/CG.2/87-1, dated: 13.5.1989. Though this pattern is not uniform across the country, their functions are similar except accepting deposits from members. They are referred to as PACBs here. The Primary Societies which are functioning in the hilly regions are named as Large Sized Agricultural Multipurpose Societies (LAMPS). The Primary Societies, which are functioning in plains and involved in multi-activities, are named as Farmers Service Societies (FSS) (Ravichandran: 2000).

2) In India, The first effort to organize The Land Mortgage Banks was made at Jhang, Punjab as early as 1920. Based on the recommendations of AIRCSC 1954 and AIRCRC 1969 the nomenclatures of these banks were changed as Primary Land Development

Banks. Again during late 1990s, they were renamed as Primary Agriculture and Rural Development Banks. As far as Tamil Nadu is concerned, these banks are functioning with new nomenclature since 15.12.1999 based on the 50th Act of 1999 Published in the Special G.O. of Tamil Nadu Government Ms. No.943.

Bibliography

Books

1. Arun Kumar.A.V., (1997), *Rural Industrialisation in India,* M.D.Publications Pvt Ltd., NewDelhi
2. Devendra Kumar Thakar, (1999), *Rural Sector Development,* Deep and Deep Publishing Pvt Ltd.. New Delhi.
3. Jay Narayan Viyas, (1986), *SSI – Hand Book,* N.K. Viyas Publishers, Ahamedabad.
4. Jayraman. B. et.al., (2002) *Rural Non-Farm Investments, An Impact Assessment,* NABARD, Mumbai.
5. Jhingan, M.L., (1994), *The Economic Development and Planning,* Konark Publishers Pvt Ltd., New Delhi.
6. Koteswara Rao, (2000), *Rural Employment – The Non-Farm Sector,* Deep and Deep Publishers Pvt Ltd., New Delhi.
7. Kulandaisamy, V., (2002), *Text Book of Cooperative Management,* Arudra Academy, Coimbatore.
8. Mehla, A.S., (1989), *Industrial Growth and Regional Development in India,* Printwell Publishers, Jaipur.

9. Nakkiran, S., (2002), *A Treatise on Cooperative Management*, Rainbow Publications, Coimbatore.

10. Papola, T.S., (1982), *Rural Industrialization—Approaches and Potentialities*, Himalaya Publishing House, Bombay.

11. Ravichandran, K., (2003), *Non-Farm Sector Loans-Innovative Approaches and Challenges in Rural Credit edited by James Mathew*, Nirmala Academic and Research Publication, Muvathupuzha.

12. Singh, B.N.P, and Debendra, K., (ed.), (1998) *Indian Economy After 50 Years of Independence, Experience and Challenges*, Vol. V, Deep and Deep Publishing House, New Delhi.

13. Thomas Fisher and Vijai Mahahan,(1997), *The Forgotten Sector, Non-Farm Employment and Enterprises in rural India*, Oxford & IBH Publishing Company, New Delhi.

14. Vasant Desai, (2000), *Small Scale Industries and Entrepreneurship*, Himalaya Publishing House, New Delhi.

15. Veena Bhatnagar, (1995), *Small Scale Industries—Concept, Status and Policy*, Kaveri Books, New Delhi.

Journals

1. Ajantha, B. Rajkonwar (2004), Cluster Approach for Developing Rural Entrepreneurship, *Yojana*, Vol. 48, No.48, March.

2. Ananth, K.H., Jayasheela and V.K. Palanna (2003), Non-Farm Production for Reduction of Poverty, *Social Welfare*, Vol. 49, No. 10.

3. Asis Roy and Salil Kumar Mukhopadhyay (2005), An Integrated Summary of NSS Fifty Fifth Round (July 1999-June 2000) Survey Results on Informal Sector Employment in India, *Sarvekshana* 88th issue Vol. 25, No. 4 and Vol. 26, No. 1, October.

4. Balasubramanya, M.H. (2005), SSI Energy Consumption Economics in Karnataka, *NCAER Margin*, Vol. 37, No. 4, July-September.

5. Bheemappa, A. (2002), Technology and Rural Industrialization, *Yojana*, Vol. 46.

6. Boothalingam, M., (1995), Rural non-farm sector and Cooperatives-A case study of Karnataka State Cooperative Agricultural and Rural Development Bank, *Land Bank Journal*, Vol. 33, June.

7. Chauhan, S.P., (1994), Employment and Food Security Through Employment-An Evaluation, *Yojana*, Vol. 38, No. 23.

8. Chidambaram, R.M., (2004), Management of Rural Employment-Bankers' Role, *Jagriti*, Vol. 48, No. 4, March.

9. Dinesh, K. Marothia (1996), Rural Non-Farm Employment, Indian Journal of Agriculture, Vol.51, No. 1 and 2, Jan-June.

10. Goswami Bora (1970), Demand for Labour in Rural Assam—A Case Study in Nowong District, *Indian Journal of Agricultural Economics*, Vol. 25, No. 3.

11. Indira Hirway (2005), Understanding Neglected Sector- Rural Transformation in India: The Role of Non-Farm Sector, *Economic and Political Weekly*, Vol.25, No. 18.

12. Jayasheela et, al (2003), Non-Farm Production for Reduction of Rural Poverty, *Social Welfare*, January.

13. Karmakar, K.G. and G.D. Banerjee (2004), Agro Processing Idustries: A Link Between Agriculture and Industry, *IASSI Quarterly*, Vol 22, No 3, Jan-March.

14. Kaveri, V.S., (2003), Strategies to Strengthening Borrower – Bank relationship in SSI. Sector, *Vinimaya*, Vol. 23, No. 1.

15. Kishore, C. Samal (1997), Rural Non-farm Activities in Specific Regions of Orissa, *Journal of Rural Development*, Vol. 16, No. 3.

16. Lanjouw, Peter & Abusaleh Shariff (2004), Rural Non-Farm Employment in India, Access, Incomes and Poverty Impact, *Economic and Political Weekly,* Vol. 39, No. 40, October.
17. Mahabub Hossain (2004), Rural Non-Farm Economy, Evidence from Household Survey, *Economic and Political Weekly,* Vol. 39, No. 36, September.
18. Mirdul, Eapan (1996), Rural Non-Farm Employment some reflections on Petty Production, *Economic and Political Weekly,* Vol. 31, No. 26, June.
19. Misra, V.N. (2000), Role of Female Labour Force Participation in Rural Poverty and Non-Farm Employment- Indian Experience, *The Indian Journal of Labour Economics,* Vol. 43, No. 2, April-June.
20. Mridul, Eapen (1994), Rural Non-Agricultural Employment in Kerala Some Emerging Tendencies, *Economic and Political Weekly,* Vol. 29, No. 21, May.
21. Nagaiya, D. (1999), Rural Non-Farm Sector in Andhra Pradesh—Trends and Directions for Future, *Journal of Rural Development,* Vol. 18, No. 11.
22. Nagendra Babu K. (2005), Evaluation of Recovery Performance in Regional Rural Banks: A Case Study, *Southern Economist,* Vol. 44, No. 2, May.
23. Namasivayam. D., (2001), The Role of Subsides in Investments—Preference of Group Members in Non-Farm Projects, *Journal of Rural Development,* Vol. 20, No. 3, October.
24. Panda, B. (1999), Growth, Composition and Determinants of Rural Non-Farm Employment in Arunachal Pradesh, *The Indian Journal of Labour Economics,* Vol. 42, No. 2.
25. Pandey, H.K., (1957), Pattern of Employment of Agricultural Labour in Uttar Pradesh, *Indian Journal of Agricultural Economics,* Vol. 12, No. 20.
26. Parthasarathy et al (1998), Determinants of Rural Non-Agricultural Employment: The Indian Case,

Indian Journal of Agricultural Economics, Vol. 53, No. 2, April-June.

27. Premaratne S.P and SMP Senanayake (2004), Access to Rural Non-Farm Economic Activities: Result from Field Study in Sri Lanka, *Indian Journal of Agricultural Economics,* Vol. 59, No. 4, December.
28. Rana Bijoy Deb (2004), Employment Generation in Small Units: A Case Study, *Yojana,* Vol. 48, May.
29. Ranjit Singh Ghuman (2005), Rural Non-Farm Employment Scenario—Reflection from Recent Data in Punjab, *Economic and Political Weekly,* Vol. 25, No. 41, October.
30. Ravindra Prabu and C. Thangamuthu (2003), Non Farm Employment among Schedule Caste Household in Tamilnadu: A Study, *Southern Economist,* Vol. 42, No. 9, September.
31. Rohilla, B.S. (1996), Initiative of NABARD for Rural Non-Agricultural Financing and Development, *The Cooperator,* Vol. 34, No. 1, July.
32. Sahoo, B.B. (2005), Primary Lending Institutions and Rural Credit Evolution, Growth and Challenges, *Kurukshetra,* Vol. 54, No. 2, December.
33. Sandeep Singh (1995), Advantages and Structural Weaknesses of Rural Industries in India, *Kurukshetra,* Vol. 28, No. 12, September.
34. Satyendra, P. Gupta (1996), Possibilities of Rural Development Through On-Farm and Non-Farm Employment—An Economic Evaluation, *Land Bank Journal,* Vol. 20, No. 3.
35. Sreeramulu. D. (2004) Growth and Overall Performance of Indian Small Scale Enterprises, *Indian Economic Panorama,* Vol. 13, No. 4, January.
36. Sudhakar Reddy, (2000), Rural Non-Farm Employment in Developing Economies: Theoretical Formulation and Empirical Evidence, *Journal for Rural Development,* Vol. 19, No. 1.

37. Suhag, K.S. et.al., (2004) Credit Delinquency in State Cooperative Land Development Bank—A Study in Haryana, *Indian Economic Panorama,* Vol. 14, No. 2, July.

38. Thorat, Y.S.P. (2006), Rural Credit in India: Issues and Concerns, *Indian Journal of Agriculture Economics,* Vol. 61, No. 1, Jan-March.

39. Tripathy, K.K., (2004), Cooperative Credit in Rural India, *Yojana,* Vol. 48, No. 4, April.

40. Unni Jeemol (1998), Non-Agricultural Employment and Poverty in Rural India – Review of Evidences, Economic and Political Weekly, Vol.33, No 13, March.

41. Unni Jeemol. (1998), Non- Agriculture Employment and Poverty in Rural India, Economic and Political Weekly, Vol.33, No.13, March.

42. Vyasalu.Vinod (1992), The NFS in Indian Economy towards a long term Research Programme in Rural Industrialization, RBI Endowment Unit, ISEC, Bangalore.

Reports

1. Government of India (2006) Report on the Task Force on Revival of Cooperative Credit Institutions (Long Term).

2. NABARD (2001), An Ex-post Evaluation Study on Rural Non-Farm Sector in Ludhiyana and Sangrur Districts of Panjab, NABARD Regional Office, Chandigarh.

3. NABARD (2003) An Evaluation Study Series No13, DRIP in Tirunelveli District, Regional Office, Chennai.

4. NABARD (2004), An Ex-post Evaluation Study on Rural Non-Farm Sector Activities in Kollom and Alappuzha Districts of Kerela, Kerela Regional Office, Thiruvandram.

5. NABARD (2004), Study Report on Employment Generation Health and Sustainability of RNFS Units

in Shimoga District, Karnataka Regional Office. Bangalore.

6. NABARD (2004-05), State Level Credit Seminar, State Focus Paper, Tamilnadu, Regional Office, Chennai.
7. NABARD (2005), An Ex-post Evaluation Study (II) on Rural Non-Farm Sector Investments in East Gothavari and Karnool District of A.P. Andhra Pradesh, Regional Office, Hyderabad.
8. NABARD (2005), An Ex-post Evaluation Study on Rural Non-Farm Sector Investments in A.P. Andhra Pradesh, Regional Office, Hyderabad.
9. NABARD (2006), Potential Linked Credit Plan for Nagapattinam District
10. NABARD (2006), Potential Linked Credit Plan for Dindugal District
11. NCUI (2004), Background Papers, 14th Indian Cooperative Congress, New Delhi.
12. Ramachandraiah G. (2002), Institutional and Infrastructural Impediments in Rural Industrialization in Dindugal District, Tamil Nadu, Research Report Series – 43, National Institute of Rural Development, Hyderabad.
13. Sharma K.C et, al., (2001), Recovery Management in Rural Credit, Occasional Paper 21, NABARD, Mumbai.
14. Subrahmanyam K.V (2000), Linkages between Farm and Non-Farm Sector-Role of Processing of Horticulture Products, Occasional Paper 16, NABARD, Mumbai.
15. Surjit Singh, (1996), Rural Non-Farm Sector in Rajasthan, Some Empirical Findings, Institution of Development Studies, Jaipur.
16. TNSCARD Bank (2002), Status Paper on NFS Financing by Agriculture and Rural Development Bank in Tamilnadu, Chennai.
17. Uzha Tuteja (2004), Rural Non-farm Employment

in Haryana, Economic Research Centre, University of Delhi.

Web References

1. Amit Mukherjee and Xiaobozhang (2005), Rural Non-Farm Development in China and India: The Role of Policies and Institution, www.ifpri.org
2. Coppard Dankl (2001) The Rural Non-farm Economy in India: A Review of the Literature NRI Report 2662. U.K, www.nri.org/rnfe/index
3. Davis Junior and Pearce Douglas, (2001), The Non-Agricultural Rural Sector in Central and Eastern Europe. NRI Report 2630 U.K. www.nri.org/work/rnfl-transition.html.
4. GOI (2005) Provisional Result of Economic Census 2005, All India Report, www.mospi.gov.in
5. Lanjouw & Peter Lanjouw (1995), Rural Non – Farm Employment of Survey, www.nri.org.
6. Saxena N.C (2003), The Rural Non-farm Economy in India: Some Policy Issues NRI Report 2752, U.K. www.nri.org/rnfe/index
7. Tiago Wandschneider and Davis Junior, (2003), Best Practice and Strategies for Promoting Rural Non-Farm Employment through Project Interventions, NRI Report 2756. U.K. www.nri./rnfe/index.html

Chart 1.2

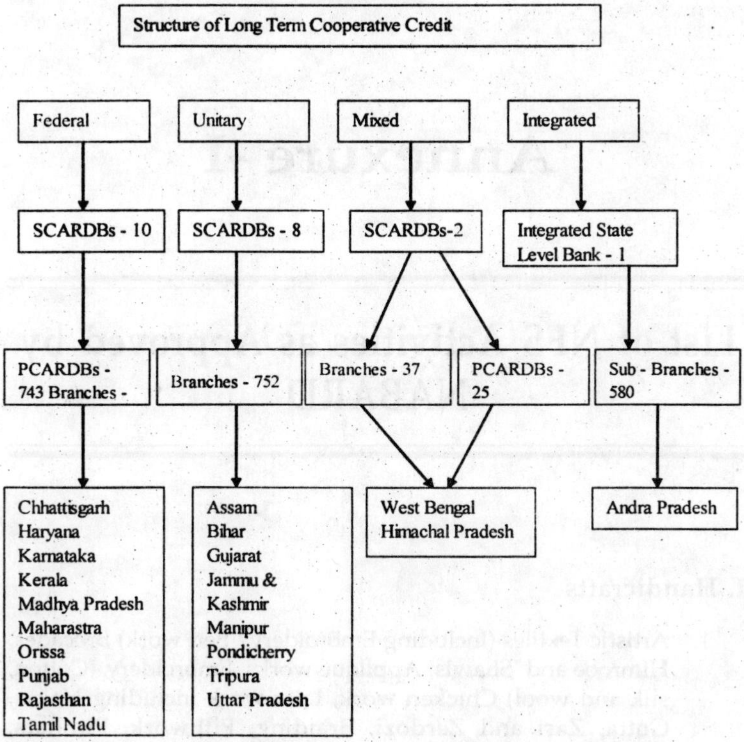

Note

1. LTCCS outlests in the States of Uttranchal and Jharkhand included in UP and Bihar respectively.
2. In the North Eastern States of Meghalaya, Nagaland, Mizoram, Arunachal Pradesh, Sikkim and in the States of Delhi, Goa, Andaman Nicobar there is no separate LTCCS. The SCBs in these states purvey both ST and LT credit.

Annexure -I

List of NFS Activities as Approved by NABARD

I. Handicrafts

1. Artistic Textiles (Including Embroidery/ Seri work) Brocades, Himrooe and Shawls. Applique works, Embroidery, (Cotton, silk and wool) Chicken work, Lace work including Nakki, Gotta, Zari and Zerdozi, Braiding, Pithwork, Pithhats, Garlands, Flowers.
2. *Bangles and Beads:* Oxidised Bangles, Bracelets, Cultured pearls.
3. *Cane Bamboo, Straw etc.:* Woodern combs, Basket making, Art Plate Manufacture.
4. *Carpets:* Wollen carpets, Rugs and Druggets including Namdhas, Gubbas and Durries, Nasnads, Sisal Rugs.
5. *Ceramice:* Earthenwares, Cjinewares.
6. *Conch shell:* Articles made of conch shell .
7. *Flax and Fiber:* Articles made of Flax and Fiber like Bags, Mats making.
8. *Hand Printing:* Hand Printing, Calico Printing, Traditional dyeing of textiles including Kslamkari, Batik, Rogan.
9. *Jewellery:* Precious, Semiprecious and Synthetic stones, Jewellery of precious metals, Imitation jewellery, outing and polishing of Red and Artificial Gems/Stones.

10. *Netsilware:* Silverwares, Bidri, Filigreee, Brassware, Copperware, Bronze castings, Ivery crving, Iron Sheel and Hern works.
11. *Stone work:* Stone carving, Marble work, Alabaster.
12. *Woodwork:* Wood carving and Inlay work, Wood turning and Lacquerware including Nirmal, Repousse work, decorative furniture, Slate frames, Toy making etc.
13. *Paper Machie*

II. Village Industries

1. Carpentry, Saw Nills, Phywood making, Wood work, Furniture, Wooden fixtures, Chippendals.
2. Blacksmithy.
3. Bee-keeping/spiculture
4. Honey and honey products
5. Cottage matches
6. Cattage NEO Soaps
7. Kuttir Gramedyeg
8. Naddi Khadi
9. Bidi making
10. Broom making
11. Manufacture and use of manure and methane gas from cowding etc.

III. Leather Industry

1. Flaying
2. Tanning.
3. Foot wear-making
4. Charmaker
5. Leather Garments.
6. Artistic/ novelty leather items.
7. Leather goods/products like Bags, Rucksacks, Wallets, Purses, Watch Straps, Belts, Cycle Saddles, Canvas Bags & boldalls.
8. Industrial Leather gloves/belts.

IV. Pottery

1. Earthen-ware pottery.
2. Decorative pottery

3. Porcelain, Chinaware.
4. Clay moulding.
5. Stoneware.
6. Rangiganj/ Mangalore tiles.
7. Artistic/noveltry pottery.
8. Fuel-efficient Chulhas.

V. Paper Products

1. Tissue Paper
2. Waxed Paper
3. Paper Bag, Envelopes
4. Paper plates, cups
5. Paper napkins.
6. Facial tissue napkins
7. Teleprinter Rolls.
8. Toilet paper rolls.
9. File covers, File Beards, Writing Pade.
10. Decorative paper.

VI. Printing, Book Binding, Lithography

VI. Glass

1. Glass ceramics
2. Glass Mirrors
3. Glass Bengles
4. Glass Beads
5. Glass slides
6. Thermometers.

VIII. Rubber Goods & Related Products

1. Foot wear/ sport shoes.
2. Cycle tyre/tubes
3. Surgical Gloves/late
4. Rubber tubes
5. Electrical wires (Insulated)
6. Paint brushes.
7. Hair brushes
8. Tooth brushes.

IX. Construction / Building Material

1. Stone crushing
2. Querrying
3. Concrete goods
4. Bricks & Tills
5. Marble works
6. Lime
7. Cement works
8. Mining
9. Chalk making
10. Sandlime tiles
11. Blocks, jallies etc.

X. Chemicals/ Chemical Products

1. Wax candles
2. Napthalene balls
3. Shoe polish
4. Wood Polish
5. French Polich
6. Metal Polish
7. Tlilet soap
8. Laundry soap
9. Tooth paste
10. Tooth powder
11. Safety matches
12. Fire works
13. Pharmaceuticals
14. Animal glue
15. Office gum paste
16. Agarbathis
17. Perfumary
18. Cologne
19. Cold Creams
20. Talcum powder
21. Toiletry
22. Soda

23. Salt
24. Industrial adhesives based on sterch/dextrin and siligates.

XI. Petrochemicals (Plastic) Products

1. PP /HD /HMPE /LDPE /LLDE films & related products.
2. PVC Granules
3. Injection mouldings, Thermoplasting products etc. Buckets, Boxes, Tube, Bags, Folders etc.
4. Polyethene sacks/ Bags
5. Other Plastic Products.

XII. General Engineerings

1. Umbrella handles
2. Conduit pipes
3. Foundries
4. Non-ferrous metal works
5. Steel trunks
6. Sheet metal works
7. Locksmithy
8. Tin smithy
9. Blacksmithy
10. Metal rolling
11. Aluminium goods
12. Postal seals
13. Brass/ copper/ bell metal works
14. Agricultural implements
15. Beam scales
16. Mechanical toys
17. Tools manufacture
18. Assembly works
19. Steve pins, safety pins
20. Aluminium buttons
21. Signal lamps
22. Hurricane lanterns
23. Barbed wire
24. Spoons – cutlery
25. forks

26. Domestic utensils-Brass, Aluminium, Copper, Iron, Silver, Bro German silver.
27. Wire Gauze.
28. Welded wire mesh
29. Razors
30. Knives & Shaving Blades
31. Bard saw blades, Chissels
32. Bottle washers / cleaners
33. Metallic Watch Straps
34. Aluminium/ Steel furniture
35. zi. Fasterners
36. Looks

XIII. Electronic/ Automobile Engineering

1. Electronical accessories
2. Radio accessories
3. Motor parts Manufacture
4. Cycle chains, mudguards
5. Cycle dynamo
6. Boosters
7. PVC wires/ soldering wires
8. Decoration bulb
9. Amplifiers for entertainment
10. Public address systems
11. Battery eliminators/ Regulators
12. Hearing aids.
13. Stators for fluorescent lamps
14. Battery chargers
15. Mini Transformers
16. Burglar Alarm

XIV. Sports Goods

1. All types of sports nets
2. Shuttle cooks
3. Hockey sticks
4. Protective equipment like pads, gloves etc.
5. Cricket bats, cricket and Hockey balls

6. Foot ball, Volley ball and Basket Ball covers
7. Physical fitness equipment

XV. Stationeary Items

1. Ink manufacture
2. Ball point pens
3. Fountain pens
4. Pen nibs
5. Pencils
6. Paper pins
7. Carbon paper
8. Hand made paper
9. Handmade cardboard
10. Drawing boards
11. Flat rules

XVI. Agro Industries

A. Agro-Input Manufacture

Eg. Chemicals, fertilizers, Manure etc.

B. Agricultural Machinery

Eg. Ploughs, cultivators, chaff cutters, disc harrows insecticide dusters/ sprayers, levelers, weeders etc.

C. Agro Processing (Including Food Processing Units)

1. Oil industry-Chani oil, NEO\
2. Hand pounding of paddy and cereals
3. Rice milling
4. Flour mills
5. Cane our & khandsari unit-Gur, khandsari
6. Palm Gur and other palm products

(a) Neera

(b) Palm sugar

(c) Palm candy

(d) Palm leaf mats/other products
(e) Palm fibre brushes

D. Food Processing (Formulations)

1. Fruit processing and preservations
2. Canning of fruits and vegetables
3. Cocoa/ Cashew nut processing
4. Tamarind processing]
5. Farsan / snacks
6. Pickles and chutneys/ saucea / ketenups/ jems
7. Spices, condiments and curry powder
8. Apphalam, papad making
9. Soups and noodles
10. Vermicelli and macaroni
11. Processing of marine products
12. Bakeries

XVII. Tailoring and Ready Made Garments

1. Hosiery
2. Garment making
3. Knitting and Tailoring
4. Upholstery etc.

XVIII. Sericulture

1. Roaring and Rooting in non-mulberry sector for production of or muga & Tasar.
2. Reasing, Reeling and Twisting and Weaving activities in mulberry sector

XIX. Coir- Coir Mats, Coir Fibres, Coir Ropes

XX. Handlooms/Power Looms

1. Manufacture of Yarn
2. Spinning
3. Cotton silk and Wool textiles
4. Lokvastra
5. Polyvastra

XXI. Activities Based on Trible/ Forest Areas

1. Collection / Processing /Marketing of Fruits, Plants, Seeds, Leaves.
2. Oil Extraction from Oil seeds of Tree origin.
3. Distillation of flowers.
4. Honey Extraction.
5. Extraction of fiber from different sources.
6. Grass, Cane, Bamboo based crafts.
7. Wood crafts.
8. Earthen ports for social forestry plants
9. Katha preparation.
10. Collection/ processing of gum, resine.
11. Collection processing of lad.
12. Other products

XXII. Service Oriented Establishments

1. Pumpsets (Electrical/ Diesel) repairing.
2. Electrical wiring/ repairing.
3. Auto mobile/ Scootor/ Motor Cycle/ Tractor repairing.
4. Repairing/ Maintenance of consumer durables.
5. Laundry eroxing and grindling services.

NB: The list is only illustrative and not exhaustive

Performance of Primary Cooperative Agriculture and Rural Development Banks in Dindugal and Nagapattinam Districts with Special reference to Non-Farm Sector Loans

Interview Schedule for Respondents

I. DEMOGRAPHY

1. Name of the Respondent : ______________________
2. Address of the Respondent : ______________________
____
____

3. Sex Male – 1 Female – 2 ☐
4. Age (Number of Completed years) ☐☐

II. SOCIAL

5. Community SC – 1, ST – 2, MBC – 3, BC – 4, FC – 5 ☐
6. Number of years you have taken to complete the education ☐☐
7. Marital Status
0 – Unmarried, 1 – Married, 2 – Widowed, 3 Divorced ☐
8. Type of family 1 – Joint, 2 – Nuclear ☐
9. Total number of members in the family ☐☐
a. No. of dependents in the family ☐☐
b. No. of earning members in the family ☐☐
10. Are you a migrant *(if no skip to question 12)*
0 – No. 1 – With in the District
2 – Other District 3 – Other State ☐
11. What is the reason for migration?
1. Monsoon failure 2. Burden of Financial Problem
3. Business loss 4. Others ☐

a) Exposure to Mass – Media

12. Do you read the following?
Journals – 4, Magazines – 3, Books – 2, Newspaper – 1
None – 0 ☐
13. How often do you watch TV?
Regularly – 3, Occasionally – 2, Rarely – 1, Never – 0 ☐
14. How often do you listen to radio?
Regularly – 3, Occasionally – 2, Rarely – 1, Never – 0 ☐

b) Contact with Change agents

(The investigator use 1 for 'Yes' and 0 for 'No')

15. Do the Govt. officials come to your village to meet the public?
Yes / No ☐

☐

16. **Do Non – Govt. officials come to your villages to meet public?**
Yes / No

17. **Have you met any of them at any time?**
Yes / No ***(if answer is no skip to Q. No. 19)***

18. **In a month how many times you are meeting them?**
Daily – 1, Weekly – 2, Occasionally – 3

c) Membership

19. **Are you a member of any following institution?**

Sl. No.	Organization	Yes – 1 No – 0	How long?	Remarks if any
Social				
1.	PACB			
2.	PARDB			
3.	SHG			
General				
1.	Religious			
2.	Political			
3.	Local Clubs			
4.	Cultural Organizations			
5.	Traders association			
6.	Any other (specify)			

III. ECONOMIC STATUS

a) Occupation

20. **What is your Occupation?**

Primary : ☐ **Secondary :** ☐

a. Farm b. NFS (Specify) ________ c. Others (Specify) ________

b) Income

21. **What is your monthly income?**

a. Agriculture : ________

b. NFS : ________

c. Others : ________ **Rs.**

22. **Extend of Agriculture land (in acres) ________**

23. **Whether your land supplies raw materials for your business?**
0 – No, 1 – Yes
(If yes Specify) ________

23. Family income per month **Rs.**

c. Expenditure

25. What is your monthly family expenditure? **Rs.**

26. Do NFS enhance your Farm income?
0 – No, 1 – Yes, ***if yes Specify*** ________________

27. What is your average monthly expenditure on Non-Farm activity?

Sl. No.	Items	Amount Spent
1.	Electricity	
2.	Interest	
3.	Rent	
4.	Wage / Salary	
5.	Telephone	
6.	Advertisement	
7.	Tax if any	
8.	Others	
	Total	

28. Where do you borrow if additional amount required?
1 – Commercial Bank, 2 – Coop. Bank, 3 - Money Lenders 4. Others

d. Savings

29. Which institution do you have deposit?
1. Cooperative, 2 Commercial, 3 Post – Office, 4 others, 5 none

30. Mention the type and amount of deposits made

1. SB, 2. RD, 3 FD, 4 CD

31. Why did you prefer this institution to save?

1. Nearer to residence, 2. Personal Contact,
3. Higher interest rate, 4.Saftey, 5. Other

e. Assets

32. Value of Assets

1. House hold assets **Rs.**

2. Land Assets **Rs.**

IV. PROFILE OF NON-FARM SECTOR

33. Nature of Occupation : 1. Traditional, 2. First Generation

34. Type of ownership 1. Sole Proprietor 2. Partnership

35. What is your father's Occupation?: ________________

36. Name of the Enterprise : ________________

37. Location of the enterprise : ________________

38. Ownership of the shop : 1 Owned 2. Rented

39. What is the reason for starting business here?

S. No.	Reasons	Yes – 1, No – 0	Remarks
1.	Availability of Raw material		
2.	Marketability		
3.	Financial Support		
4.	Support of Relatives		
5.	Transport Facility		
6.	Any other (Specify)		

40. Do you think that NFS is more remunerative than agriculture?
Yes – 1, No – 0

41. If yes, What makes it more remunerative than agriculture?
1. Assured income 2. Less Expensive
3. Less risk 4. Carried on throughput the year

42. Whether your enterprise is registered under SSI :

43. Did you have any previous experience in this field?
If yes, How many years
1. Below 6 months 2. 6 months to 1 year
3. 1 to 2 years 4. 2 years and above

44. Have you undergone any training before starting the present enterprise?
1 Yes , 0 – No.
If yes, mention the training organization
1. SISI, 2 CED, 3 DIC, 4 Nationalized Banks, 5 other

45. Have you got any training after starting enterprise?

46. Do you need any additional training for your business?

47. If NFS is a primary occupation, why did you choose this NFS activity?
1. To earn more income
2. To generate employment opportunity to others
3. Government provided subsidized loan
4. To stabilize farm income
5. Neighbours have started NFS activity
6. Others

48. If you are doing NFS as secondary occupation what are the reasons?
1. To stabilize farm income
2. Land become arable
3. Continuous drought
4. The availability of input for NFS from agricultu.e.
5. The availability of cattle
6. Availability of marketing facility
7. Availability of skills
8. Availability of labour

9. Other (Specify) ______________

V. MOTIVATIONAL FACTORS

49. Who motivated you to start this NFS activity?
    1. On your own accord 2. Government Official
    3. Commercial Banking personnel 4. Friends & Relatives
    6. Others (Specify) ______________

50. What motivated you to start NFS activity?
    1. To earn income 2. To generate employment for you
    3. To generate employment for your spouse
    4. To generate employment for others
    5. Role model to others
    6. To earn social status

VI. INVESTMENTS

51. What is your initial investment in NFS Rs. [| | |]

    Working Capital Rs. [| | |]

52. How did you mobilize fund for NFS activity? [ ]
    1. Own savings 2. Borrowings 3. Both

VII. BORROWINGS

53. From whom did you borrow and how much?

Sl. No.	Items	Amount Borrowed (Rs)	Interest (Rs)	Outstanding (Rs)
1.	PARDB			
2.	Commercial Bank			
3.	Private Money Lenders			
4.	Friends and Relatives			
5.	Others (Specify)			
	Total			

54. Why did you choose this organization to borrow loan? [ ]
    1. Low rate of interest 2. Accessibility 3. Nearness
    4. Quick sanction of loan 5. Easy terms and conditions 6. Others

55. Mode of loan disbursement. How many installments? [ ]

56. Time lag for receiving loan amount [ ]
    1. 15 days 2. 15 – 16 days 3. 1 months and above

57. What security did you offer to get loan? [ ]
    1. Land 2. Assets purchased out of loan 3. House / Plot
    4. Jewels 5. Others (Specify) ______________

58. What is the period of loan ? (in months) [ ]
    1. up to 1 year 2. One year to three years
    3. 3 years to 5 years 4. Five years and above

59. What is the annual rate of interest? (in percent) [|]

60. What is the mode of repayment?
 1. Monthly2. Quarterly 3. Annually

61. What are the advantages of getting loans from institutional agencies?
 1. Low rate of interest 2. Easy installments
 3. Availability of loan in time
 4. Availability of loan required amount 5. others ________

62. What are the problems you have faced while borrowing?
 1. Cumbersome procedure 2. Time consuming process
 3. Lack of Public Relations with the employees
 4. Delay in sanctioning of loans
 5. High incidental charge 6. High down payment
 7. Others ________ 7. None

63. Whether you have borrowed from more than one agency?
 1. Yes 0. No

64. Whether you have borrowed loan in the name of your spouse?
 If yes, in which institution?
 0 – None, 1 – Cooperative Bank, 2 – Commercial Bank 3 – Others

65. If yes, give details of loan borrowed in the name of your spouse

Purpose	Amount	Rate of interest

VIII. UTILIZATION OF LOANS

66. Have you fully utilized the loan amount for the purpose for which it was borrowed? 1 – Yes, 0 – No

67. If yes,
 1. Loan was available in time
 2. Supervision of bank officials
 3. Adequacy of loan
 4. Others ________

68. If no, Why?
 1. Delay in getting loans
 2. Urgent expenditure
 3. The cost of project increased due to price escalation
 4. Others ________

69. Whether any supervision over the utilization of loan?
 0 – No, 1 – Yes

70. If yes, how many times?
 1. Daily 2. Weekly 3. Monthly 4. Quarterly 5. Half yearly 6. Yearly

IX. REPAYMENT

71. What is the extent of loan repaid?
 1. Fully paid 2. Partially paid 3. Not yet repaid

72. If fully paid, what are the reasons?
 1. Good income from investment 2. Productive use of loan

3. To get next loan 4. To maintain credibility
5. Pressure from bankers 6. Others ________

73. If partially paid, what are the reasons?
1. Lesser income 2. unexpected expenses
3. Installment remaining 4. Money used for consumption purposes
5. Others ________

74. If partially paid, how many installments pending?

75. If loan is unpaid, what are the reasons?
1. Low income 2. inefficient business practices
3. Heavy operating expenses 4. High cost of raw materials
5. Lesser demand for product 6. Others ________

X. PROFILE OF PRODUCT / SERVICE

76. What are the products you have produced ? ________

77. Do you have Brand name?
0 – No, 1 – Yes

78. Why did you choose the product?
1. Easy availability of raw materials 2. Marketability
3. Low cost of production 4. Others ________

79. Whether your product is eco – friendly?
0 – No. 1 – Yes

80. Do you have quality certificates for your product?
1. AGMARK 2. ISI 3. ISO 4. Others ________

a. Technology

81. Whether the technology used in your business is imported?

82. Cost of technology implementation

b. Marketing

83. What is your market area?
1. Local 2. Other District 3. Other State 4. Export / Overseas

84. To whom you market your service / products?
1. Government 2. Organizations 3. Individuals 4. Traders
5. More than one

85. Why do you choose this segment of consumers to market your products?
1. Better price 2. Transport facilities
3. Prompt payment 4. Others ________

86. What is your pricing strategy?
1. Cost plus pricing
2. Active price policy
3. Seasonal price policy
4. Others ________

87. How do you maintain distribution network?
1. Appointing dealers

2. Cash and carry system
3. Contacting directly buses or lorries
4. Others ____________

88. What is the arrangement made for transport?
1. Own vehicles 2. Hired vehicles on contract
3. Using regular buses or lorries
4. does not arise

89. Do you have godown facilities ? 0 – No, 1 – Yes

90. If yes, what is the cost of godown

c. Management

91. Role in management of the unit
1. Holding top position
2. Looking after sub – functions only
3. Policy making only

92. Decision making in your business
1. Always own decision 2. Husband / Wife domination
3. Parents 4. Partners
5. Consulting with other experts

93. Time spent in unit in a day
1. 10 and more hours 2. 6 to 9 hrs 3. 3 to 5 hrs 4. below 3 hrs

XI.EMPLOYMENT GENERATION

94. How many days in a month you are employed in NFS activity?

95. Number of people employed
1. Nil 2. Skilled
3. Semi – Skilled 4. Unskilled
5. Family members Total :

96. What is the present wage / Salary to workers per month?
1. Skilled – Rs. :
2. Semi – Skilled – Rs. :
3. Unskilled – Rs. :

97. Is there any labour turn over?
0 – No 1 Yes

98. If yes what are the reasons?
1. Inadequate wage
2. Lack of infrastructure
3. Lack of skill
4. Start their own business
5. Other Specify ____________

99. How many days in a month your employees engaged in your business?

100. Do you have any proposal to appoint employees additionally?

101. If yes, how many ?

XII. ACHIEVEMENTS

102. Did you get any awards for your business from Government / any other side?
    0 – No.   1 – Yes

103. What is the Future plan for your business?

XIII. ROLE OF GOVERNMENT

104. Do you think that Govt. schemes and programmes promoted NFS in your locality?
    0 – No.   1 - Yes

105. If yes, how
    1. By providing general awareness
    2. By providing needed training
    3. By arranging for infrastructure
    4. By arranging for marketing facilities
    5. By arranging financial facilities
    6. Others (specify) ____________

106. What are the services / support you except from Govt. for the promotion of NFS?
    1. Arranging loan at cheaper rate of interest.
    2. Establishing separate department at district level for the promotion of NFS
    3. Protecting the Indigenous / traditional entrepreneurship
    4. Others (Specify) ____________

XIV. PROBLEMS

107. Problems in setting up the unit
    1. Electrical connection   2. Delay in erection of units
    3. Lack of working capital   4. Others ____________

108. Raw materials related problems
    1. High cost   2. Problem of Transportation
    3. Delay in getting   4. Others ____________

109. Machine related problems
    1. Repairs and damages   2. Problem of supply of water and power
    3. Source of technicians   4. Others ____________

110. Problems related to institutional support
    1. Pressure from bankers   2. Additional loans are not given
    3. Lack of guidance   4. Others ____________

111. Problems related to family support
    1. Discourage from family members
    2. Lack of assistance   3. Others ____________

112. What are the problems you are facing in marketing your service / product?
    1. Increasing competition   2. Lack of packing technology
    3. No support from Government
    4. No support from lending institutions
    5. Availability of substitute service / commodity
    6. Others ____________

113. Problems related to employees

1. Labour turnover 2. High cost of labour 3. Union problem
4. Non availability of skilled labour

114. How do you overcome the problem?

115. Did you get any support from others to overcome the problem? If so give details

116. Did you have better environment for your business

If yes, how?

If no, Why?

117. What is your suggestion for the promotion of NFS activities?

SCHEDULE - II

The Performance of Primary Cooperative Agriculture and Rural Development Bank in Dindugal and Nagapattinam Districts with Special Reference to Non-form sector loans

Interview Schedule for Primary Cooperative Agriculture and Rural Development Bank

I General Information

1. Name and Address of the Bank
2. Date of Registration and Commencement of the Bank
3. Area of operation of the bank
4. Objectives of the bank
5. Eligibility for membership as per the bye laws

II. Information related to NFS

1. What are the Procedures followed for issuing loan?
2. What are the special procedures followed for NFS loan?
3. What are the types of NFS activities for which loans are provided?
4. What are the Documents required for getting NFS loan?
5. What is the loan appraisal norms followed for investment?
6. What is the normal time lag between application received and sanction of loan?
7. What is the normal time lag between sanctioning of loan and disbursement?
8. Mode of loan disbursement./ installment
9. Types of loan issued Composite loan / integrated loan.
10. Block capital or Working Capital.
11. What is rate of interest charged for NFS loan?

NABARD to SCARDB ______________
SCARD to PCARDB ______________
PCARDB to Borrowers ______________

12. How much/ margin money / Down payment charged for NFS loan.

13. What are the security needs for getting loan?

14. Repayment period – for different activities

15. Whether any Grace period/ Moratorium is given to borrowers

16. Whether any subsidy is given to borrowers.

17. Whether any entrepreneurial training is given to NFS borrowers before sanctioning loan? If Yes. Give details.

18. Whether any special recovery mechanism has been formed for collection of overdue?

19. What are the actions taken against defaulters?

20. How many time NFS unit have been visited for loan disbursement and recovery?

21. Whether any consultancy and guidance has been given to NFS borrowers? If yes, what are those?

22. Whether any marketing facilities have been arranged to NFS borrowers? If yes, give details.

23. Whether the bank has any tie-up with any other organizations or NGO for the promotion of NFS activities?

24. Do you feel that NFS loan has increased your volume of transaction?

25. Do you feel that recovery is better in NFS loan than farm loan?

    Yes / No

26. Management Structure of the bank.

III. 1. Give details on the following

Particular			00-01	01-02	02-03	03-04	04-05	05-06
Membership	A Class	Farm						
		NFS						
	B Class							
	Institutions							
	Total							
	Borrowed							
Share Capital	Authorized							
	Paid up							
Reserve fund								
Borrowings	SCARDB							
	Govt							
	Others							
Working Capital								
Investments								
Loan Issued	Farm							
	NFS							
	Others							
Loan Demand	Farm							
	NFS							
	Others							
Loan Collection	Farm							
	NFS							
	Others							
Loan overdue	Farm							
	NFS							
	Others							
Loan Outstanding	Farm							
	NFS							
	Others							
Profit / Loss								
Audit classification								
Any others								

2. Purpose wise loan recovery under NFS

Purpose	00-01	01-02	02-3	03-04	04-05	05-06

3. Purpose wise loan Demand

Purpose	00-01	01-02	02-3	03-04	04-05	05-06

4. Purpose wise loan overdue

Purpose	00-01	01-02	02-3	03-04	04-05	05-06

5. Overdue and NPA Position

	Agri	NFS	Agri	NFS	Agri	NFS	Agri	NFS	Agri	NFS	Agri	NFS
Standard												
Sub Stan												
Doubt full												
II												
III												
Unsecured												
Loss												
Total NPA												
% of NPA to Total outstanding												

6. Provision for NPA

	Agri	NFS	Agri	NFS	Agri	NFS	Agri	NFS	Agri	NFS	Agri	NFS
Sub Stan												
Doubtfull												
II												
III												
Unsecured												
Loss												
Total Provision												

Index

Working Capital 49-51
World Bank 94